FAVORITE WILDFLOWERS
OF THE GREAT LAKES
AND THE NORTHEASTERN U.S.

WRITTEN BY
DICK SCHINKEL

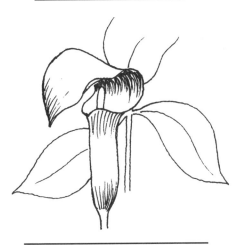

ILLUSTRATED BY
DAVID MOHRHARDT

With 100 full-color illustrations

Lansing, Michigan

Manufactured in the United States of America

94 95 96 97 98   1 2 3 4 5 6 7 8

Illustrations by David Mohrhardt
Edited by Maureen MacLaughlin Morris
Prepress by Number One Graphics
Printing by Lansing Printing
Cover design by Advanced Imaging
Logo design by Lynda A. Bass

Lansing, Michigan

ISBN 1-882376-04-8

TABLE OF CONTENTS

This book is dedicated to
Chuck Nelson
Director of the Sarett Nature Center

and

to my father, Edmund Schinkel,
who encouraged we children
to enjoy the out-of-doors
and all of its wonders.

FOREWORD

Wildflowers are different from many wild things in that they don't scurry away never to be seen again, and they are not afraid when we approach them. Wildflowers are wonderful. They are colorful, they smell good, and they are everywhere. They are an integral part of our environment appearing almost as if by magic in our backyards, neighborhoods, local parks, woods, and fields.

With a little effort, we can become acquainted with the wildflowers of our yards and neighborhoods, learn their names, and even a little more about them. You will find yourself looking forward to them each year, and will discover that you learn something new each season.

INTRODUCTION

The purpose of this book is five-fold. First, it will help you learn to identify the most common wildflowers in any neighborhood, field, yard, or park. Second, you will learn about the basic anatomy of the plant and its flowers as an aid in the identification process. Third, you will come to appreciate the role of the wildflower in the world of nature. It is exciting to realize that the Goldfinch feeding on the thistledown of the Bull Thistle could mean the young are in a nest nearby, or that perhaps the Finch is taking the thistledown to build a nest. It is fascinating to know the Teasel head will soon be getting two rings of flowers as it continues blooming, and if it is to be used in a dried fall flower arrangement we need to bring gloves in order to handle it safely.

The fourth purpose of this book is to encourage you to use these plants in your own backyards and gardens. Many of these plants can be successfully used to enhance the landscape design. Often this can be done as effortlessly as collecting seeds or digging a plant or two. However, care must be taken not to violate any laws or the integrity of another's property. Many wildflower gardeners are willing to share. Wildflower gardening is very popular and many gift catalogs exist as well as local garden shops that can take care of your needs. As this book cannot possibly cover all the wildflowers, the fifth purpose is to pique your curiosity and encourage you to learn more about other plants and wildflowers.

The wildflowers in this book are arranged according to color. For ease of identification, a colored tab in the upper right-hand corner of the color plate will permit quick location in the book. A brief description is given about the plant, flower and leaves; the conditions it needs to grow; where in the eastern United States it may be found; and, finally, information on attracting butterflies and hummingbirds. If there is any folklore behind the plant this is included, as well as how it may be used in your own landscape design.

GROWING WILDFLOWERS IN YOUR GARDEN

As in any type of gardening, much of the work and pleasure is in the planning. A few basic questions must be asked before you begin. The first and most important is: What do you want from the wildflower garden? A few things to consider are: Are you planting for flowers? for wildlife? for ground cover? for what season? for butterflies? or just for natural beauty? Once you have determined what you want from the garden, you will be able to decide which type of garden will best suit your needs.

Will your garden be a woodland spring wildflower garden or will it be a shade garden? Do you have a wet area? Would a prairie be the best type of garden to suit your needs or some combination? The soil and topography of the lot will, of course, determine the limitations and strengths of the proposed garden. Doing a soil analysis is a must in order to give you the best chance of success in growing the plants you choose.

Once you have decided what type of garden you want and what you expect of it, then you can begin to select plants that will fill your expectations and which are applicable to your situation. As much work as you can do here will save you grief and money later. This book provides some information on where to locate lists, seeds, and books on wildflower propagation.

Now a decision has to be made. How much are you willing to invest in time and money over how long? Can you design it yourself or would it be better to utilize a professional landscape designer? Do you want this done next year or can you work at it over the next five to ten years? These are hard questions that have be answered realistically to avoid disappointment. Once you have done that then set up your timetable and order! Have fun, enjoy the sweat and hard work, and most importantly, sit back and enjoy the colorful results of your labor with family and friends.

HUMMINGBIRDS AND BUTTERFLIES

Attracting hummingbirds can be a focus of the wildflower garden or just an accent of it. Hummingbirds, of course, feed on nectar from flowers, but they also must eat protein and build nests. Unfortunately, we have only one species of hummingbird in the eastern United States, the Ruby Throated Hummingbird. Most hummingbirds are attracted to red or orange flowers that have long tubes or corollas. If you plant these types of plants or wildflowers your chances are greater in attracting and keeping these tiny birds.

You should also be aware of the blooming times of the plants. Very early in the spring, red flowers may be difficult to find so the hummingbird will use other flowers, including those of the wild currant and blueberries, even though these are white. Often a succession of flowers of many kinds is better. You may wish to have ornamental plants, and even a hummingbird feeder available for times of few blooms.

Attracting butterflies has become more popular over the years and a number of books have come out on the art of butterfly watching. Recently, a video called "Attracting Butterflies to Your Backyard" was made by Michael Godfrey, cinematographer of the National Audubon's "Up Close" series. This video shows that the two plants that work best for attracting butterflies are the Butterfly Bush and Verbena Bonariensis.

It is also important to remember that the caterpillars of the butterflies must eat, and so some consideration should be given to the host plant for the particular butterfly you wish to attract. Sometimes a host plant may be shared by more than one butterfly, but more often the host plant is very specific to one butterfly. If you are going to encourage butterfly propagation, an evaluation of your pesticide program may be in order. Many pesticides are nondiscriminating, so be selective.

Beside obtaining the plants that attract butterflies, you may wish to provide water or even a puddle in sand. Another attractant is spoiling fruit or fermenting fruit juices. There are a number of butterfly feeders and hibernation boxes on the market, but they generally do not work well enough to purchase.

It is no longer in vogue to collect butterflies and mount them. It is far better to watch them and photograph them.

MARSH MARIGOLD

The Cowslip, as the Marsh Marigold is also called, can be found in wet and marshy places throughout the eastern United States. This early spring wildflower blooms from late March through May. It can reach a height of over two feet. The flowers are a couple of inches in width.

The yellow petals are not true petals, but really sepals that range from five to nine in number. The leaves are on stalks and heart-shaped with small teeth on the outer edges. The leaves are dark green and somewhat shiny, resembling the shape of a Violet or Wild Ginger leaf. As summer progresses the flower heads turn to seed pods that open. Most often the leaves then die back.

The Marsh Marigold is not easily grown in our normal landscaping because of its need for consistent moisture. However, this plant is increasingly found in water gardens and waterscapes because of its large leaves and early spring color. The Marsh Marigold has been used with greens, but not with much popularity.

One possible explanation for the name Cowslip is that it is found in wet pastures. Early farmers only grazed their cattle on waste land they could not cultivate. Cows would of course "slip" around during the spring on the wet soil.

The Marsh Marigold can be found in the shallow waters surrounding ponds and streams. Accompanying plants are the Blue Iris, Cattail, Arrowhead, and Arrow Arum.

Many early butterflies such as the Mourning Cloak will find this flower very tempting for its nectar. During the late spring migration the flowers are visited by many warblers because of the insects they attract, especially when the weather is cool. The Marsh Marigold, or Cowslip, does better in the north country where snow covers the ground.

Caltha palustris

MARSH MARIGOLD

COMMON BUTTERCUP

The Common, or Tall, Buttercup, is characterized by five yellow, glossy petals in its flower. These yellow petals, forming a cup, shine much like warm, yellow butter, thus the name Buttercup. Another Buttercup that is similar is the Swamp Buttercup, which is characteristically found in marshy areas. *Ranunculus* means "frog-like," and is part of the scientific name probably because this plant is often found where frogs prevail. The leaves are heavily dissected and usually have three sections. They resemble celery leaves.

The plant grows rather slowly early in the blooming season, but as other plant competition increases, the plants get taller and often reach several feet in height. The Common Buttercup grows in ditches, meadows, and thickets. Several varieties of Buttercup grow throughout the United States, the Common Buttercup among them.

The Buttercup is poisonous to both animals and humans and if eaten can cause serious gastric disturbances. The juices of the stem can cause skin irritation and even blisters. Cattle that eat fresh Buttercups from the pasture give a milk that tastes bad and is reddish in color. However, hay that includes the plant seems to lose the effects of the foul sap.

Long ago school children would pick a Buttercup flower, and tell you to sniff it. If your nose turned yellow they would tell you that you stole the butter.

A number of flowers related to the Buttercup are used in the backyard garden, but the Wild Buttercup is little used unless it is in concert with a natural planting for a meadow.

The Buttercup attracts spring butterflies and bees. The fact that it is associated with many violets and other low-growing plants of the rich, moist soils helps it attract bees. Swallowtails, the Blue Wing, and the small Copperwing butterflies are attracted to the bright, shiny, almost wet-looking, petals and feed upon the Buttercup in the early summer.

Ranunculus acris

COMMON BUTTERCUP

EVENING PRIMROSE

After receiving so many weedy species of plants from Europe we finally exported one to them, the Evening Primrose. It was named Primrose because its scent reminded people of the old world Primroses. The flowers of the Evening Primrose, at least in the first part of the blooming season, only open during the evening and night. It is highly scented which attracts the night-pollinating moths such as the Hawk Moth. Later in the summer and fall the flowers remain open during the day.

It is common over the eastern United States, and is found in dry fields as it is imported from our prairies and dunelands.

The Evening Primrose reaches heights of six feet. The yellow flowers are two inches in length with four petals having recurved sepals. The leaves are paired, lance-shaped, have small teeth, and may reach six to ten inches in length. The stem may be colored reddish at the top along with some of the leaves.

The seeds are produced in pods that are shaped like a banana and can be up to one inch long. Once the seed pods mature, usually during the fall and winter, they open, much like peeling a banana and the exposed seeds drop out. Goldfinches and other birds love the seeds and feed extensively upon the pods all winter long. Some have called these pods "banana birdseed."

The plant's roots are also edible during the first year of its biennial life while they are most tender. The first year of growth is used to store food energy in the root system and the second year produces the flowers and seed. The plant then dies.

The fields that have an abundance of Evening Primrose are a sight to behold in the evening as the sun sets with its golden glow hitting the tall flower stalks. Coupled with the Sweet Clovers, Common Mullien, and Queen Anne's Lace it is easy to see why old fields are called meadows instead of weed fields.

The Evening Primrose is a biennial that warrants a place in the heart of the summer natural gardener. The flowers are visited by the Fritillaries, Monarchs, and some Sulphurs. Bees and beetles like the flowers for the nectar.

Oenothera biennis

EVENING PRIMROSE

YELLOW SWEET CLOVER

As in all clovers, the Yellow Sweet Clover has three leaflets that are finely toothed. The yellow flowers are clustered on stalks at the end of the plant and at the leaf axils. White Sweet Clover is similar except the flowers are white. Both plants are common across the continent in fallow places and roadsides. These clovers can be found in any corner of a yard that has been left alone for a season. The small, round flowers bloom from spring throughout the summer. The plants may reach a height of nearly six feet.

The clovers add nitrogen to the soil by taking nitrogen from the air and converting it so that it can be utilized by other plants. All clovers, and the Yellow Sweet Clover is no exception, are heavily visited by honeybees for the rich nectar they provide. The small flowers of the Yellow Sweet Clover attract the short-mouthed honeybees. The Red and White clovers attract the longer-mouthed insects such as bumble-bees. Clover honey is much prized and many apiaries are placed around the fields to take advantage of these blossoms.

Although many bees and butterflies like the Sweet Clover for its flowers, only a few, like the tiny Blue, use it for the host plant. Occasionally, some of the Sulphurs will use the Sweet Clover for food but they actually prefer the Mustard family.

The seed pods hang onto their seeds for a good while after they are mature which makes the seeds available to birds.

This plant is not used in any normal landscape design even though the flowers are pretty. The plants are too straggly to be of much ornamental value.

Upon occasion the Yellow Sweet Clover has been used for flavorings of butter and cheese. Some cultures used the plants for greens but they were not highly prized.

Melilotus officinalis

YELLOW SWEET CLOVER

BLACK-EYED SUSAN

A common flower of waste areas and roadsides, the Black-eyed Susan belongs to the family of composites (Daisy) known as the Coneflowers. These flowers are found throughout the entire United States, usually in disturbed and sandy areas. The Black-eyed Susan is a native of the west that has invaded the eastern part of the country.

A biennial, the Black-eyed Susan, produces a basal rosette from seed its first year of growth. The second year it produces lovely two-and-one-half inch flowers. The plant then matures its seeds and dies. The yellow flower petals are varied in length and perpendicular to the central cone, which helps distinguish it from some of the other yellow Coneflowers. The central black portion of the flower gives it the 'black eye.'

Easily grown in most soil conditions, this flower can withstand some drought. However, it can become a nuisance, so caution should be used in its introduction. This plant does best in a natural meadow because it requires full sun.

The Black-eyed Susan blooms mid to late summer. Many horticultural hybrids have been developed from this plant which is more suitable for formal gardens.

The Black-eyed Susan is a striking flower when seen in a field of other wildflowers such as Queen Anne's Lace, Ox-Eye Daisy, Geradia, Clovers, Hawkweeds, and Milkweeds. Besides being a beautiful plant, it also attracts beneficial insects to the yard or field. The Black-eyed Susan is a good companion plant because these insects help protect the remaining plants in the garden.

Rudbeckia hirta

BLACK-EYED SUSAN

YELLOW HAWKWEED

Yellow Hawkweed is quite common throughout the eastern United States, with about eight different species being prevalent. The Yellow Hawkweed, like the Orange Hawkweed, is a composite, as the flowers are composed of numerous flowers in a large flower head. The flowers close at the end of each day and open the next until the seeds are set. The seeds look like small dandelion heads although they do not stay on the head as long. The plant has a basal rosette of leaves from which the flower stalk emerges. The flowers can reach one inch across and the plants can reach almost three feet tall. Other names for the Yellow Hawkweed are Cat's Ear, Mouse Ear, King Devil, and Canada Hawkweed.

This is not a plant usually cultivated in our yards. However, the Hawkweeds can be quite attractive if allowed to survive in natural borders or in those areas less conspicuous and not mown as often. Goldfinches and other birds love the seeds as they mature.

The Yellow Hawkweed is a companion plant to the rest of the Hawkweeds growing during the early part of the summer in dense fields with other meadow plants such as the Ox-Eye Daisy. If you are lucky, you may find a group of Yellow Hawkweed along with a clump of Indian Paintbrush which accent each other perfectly.

There is a legend which says that on the full moon of June when the Hawkweed is in seed, a gentle breeze will take the tiny seed parachutes off to become the new feathers of the geese as they go through their molt late in the month. Another legend states that does who make a diet of the Hawkweed in spring will have twins the following year.

Hieracium canadensis

YELLOW HAWKWEED

COMMON DANDELION

Everyone knows the Dandelion; it is the scourge of our lawns. One of the composites, the Dandelion has a yellow compound flower one to two inches across. The plant can reach a foot or more in height. The Dandelion originates from a basal rosette, and has an oblong leaf that is deeply cut with secondary teeth. The primary teeth are larger at the end of the leaf. This weed of European origin can be found over the entire United States in most soil conditions.

Most of us feel that spring is not really here until the first Dandelion blooms in early April. Dandelions continue blooming throughout the summer, although they are most prolific in spring. Within a few days the yellow flowers turn to a ping pong ball of white fluff. These balls are made of many individual seeds, each having a stalk, and a parachute which carries it to a new location where it will germinate if conditions are right. These seeds can actually be carried great distances and remain dormant for long periods of time.

Dandelions have long been used as a spring tonic. The greens have been touted as keeping all sorts of ills away when cooked or used as a salad green. The best greens are harvested during the early spring or on very young plants. The blossoms are used to make a mild, almost clear, wine which is excellent. A tasty recipe uses early leaves cooked with vinegar, bacon pieces, and mustard. Dandelions are regarded primarily as a pest in the home yard but are liked extensively for their seed by goldfinches. Rabbits like the tender, new leaves and honeybees find the early flowers a great source for nectar and pollen.

Children often pick the long-stalked flower heads and braid them into yellow crowns. A charming story exists that the flowers of the Dandelion are ground nymphs waiting to spring forward during the summer, but first must see if spring has really arrived by peering from the ground. When the sun is warm enough they then spring forward with a white cloak and disappear into the summer.

Taraxacum officinale

20

COMMON DANDELION

COMMON TANSY

The Common Tansy, a plant of the Daisy family, is easily recognized once you realize it has no flower rays. The small, yellow buttons are clustered at the top of a very tall plant, sometimes reaching up to five feet. This plant can be found throughout the entire eastern United States. It usually grows along roadsides, and in old fields, and meadows. The leaves are deeply cut and fern-like with teeth.

This European import was long used for medicinal purposes, but because of its extremely bitter and unappetizing nature it was not used extensively. This plant is also poisonous, which did not help its popularity. Probably its most extensive use today is for dried flower arrangements and natural dying. The plant gives off a variety of earthen colors depending upon when the dye "soup" is formed. The colors extracted are a yellow-green to brownish yellow.

Because of its use in the home, this plant was adapted to the home garden. Being quite tall, it provides a wonderful background for a perennial bed. The flowers remain for a long time and even the dead plants are quite attrac-tive. The Common Tansy blooms from mid-summer until October.

Indians used Tansy as an insect repellent, chopping the leaves and stems and placing them into their bedrolls and mattresses. The odor from the plant allegedly kept many insects away, but it is not known whether any true repellent exists. Perhaps just the changing of the bedding plants was of benefit. Rubbing new leaves on the skin to ward off mosquitoes is somewhat effective. As the plants become older, the need for the repellent wanes and so does the effectiveness.

Tanacetum vulgare

COMMON TANSY

SUNFLOWER

Sunflowers are one of the best examples of the composite family. This Daisy has a large, flat head of flowers surrounded by the bright, yellow, showy ray flowers. The ray flowers attract bees and other insects to pollinate the interior flowers which do not waste energy growing the fancy petals. The toothed leaves of the Sunflower are generally oblong and opposite and are sometimes rough on the surface. The Sunflower is adapted to dry and prairie-type soils, although some are found in wet areas and forests. In fact, the Sunflower can be found virtually everywhere.

Many native species exist that are much smaller than the garden variety. It may have received the name Sunflower because the flower head follows the sun as it crosses the sky, or because the flower rays make the head look like the sun.

The Sunflower has been around for along time and was used extensively by native peoples and pioneers in numerous ways. The flower heads were eaten when young, and they were also used to make a permanent yellow dye. The stems are very coarse, and were used to make all sorts of fibers. The leaves were used as a substitute for tobacco.

The Plains Indians revered the Sunflower as a sign of good times and happiness, likening it to the sun which gave them warmth and summer.

The seeds are high in protein and oils, and are still used today for cooking and in margarines. Their most popular use is in the bird feeding industry where the tiny, black, oily sunflower seed is the number one preferred food of birds.

A great number of hybrids have been produced for the home gardener. Some of these have multiple flower heads, and others have different flower colors. These new hybrids also make excellent cut flowers or dried flowers. They must be replanted each year as they are annuals.

Helianthus divaricatus

SUNFLOWER

BEGGAR-TICK

The Beggar-tick, also called Sticktights, received its name from the ability of the seed to stick to clothing. The flowers are similar to the rest of the Daisy family, having a compound head. However, the flowers of the Beggar-tick lack the large ray flowers. In place of ray flowers they have leafy bracts which are sometimes yellowish. This makes the plant resemble the Sunflower.

Growing three or four feet tall, the Beggar-tick has a compound leaf, divided pinnately into three to five lance-shaped, toothed leaves. Others of this group may have simple leaves that are similar to the leaflets. The leaves are opposite. Some flowers in this group, called Bur Marigolds, have ray flowers.

The seeds are oblong with one end being nearly square. From this end, two to four barbs with tiny hooks protrude nearly half again the length of the seed. This shape gives rise to the name Devil's Bootjack. The shape is that of a bootjack with a pitchfork. These barbs hook into the clothing or fur of any passerby, thereby relocating the seed to a new home. However, unlike the Showy Tick-trefoil, the Beggar-tick will ride upon its host for a long time and hopefully a long distance. This gives the Beggar-tick an advantage in dispersal into other habitats. Other names for this plant are Pitchforks, Stick-seed, Harvest Lice, Cow Lice, and Spanish Needles.

The Beggar-ticks like soil that is moist and it grows along marshes, streamsides, shorelines, and ditches. Because of this growth habit, duck hunters and their dogs are prone to having a handsome collection of these seeds. Found throughout the United States everyone has experienced these as extra baggage.

Not used in our gardens, these plants should be eliminated. In the wild, some birds will make use of the seeds as they are high in energy and protein.

Bidens frondosa

BEGGAR-TICK

GOATSBEARD

This tall, yellow flower is found throughout the eastern United States, except in the very southern states. It is sometimes called Meadow Salsify and has grass-like leaves that clasp the stem. The Yellow Goatsbeard grows about three feet tall, and the flower heads get as large as two-and-one-half inches across.

Many children call this composite a Giant Dandelion as the seed head appears similar with its seed parachutes. The giant puff-balls are used in dried flower arrangements with the seeds being kept intact with a covering of hair spray, or a few carefully placed drops of super glue.

The Goatsbeard blooms in waste places, roadsides, and meadows from mid-summer through the fall. The flowers close up during the afternoon and during cloudy weather. Indians used its congealed sap for chewing. The roots can be used as a cooked vegetable and the leaves as greens.

There are other differently-colored Goatsbeards found throughout the United States. Some of these may hybridize. The Goatsbeards are not culti-vated to any extent, but can be an attractive asset to a natural garden setting when found as a volunteer.

The Indians and early settlers viewed the Goatsbeard as just a giant Dandelion and tried to use it in the same manner as food. They were unsuccessful because of the difference in taste. Other Indians thought that the seeds of the Goatsbeard were the spirits of the summer run of river suckers, which usually came about the same time the seeds were dispersed.

Tragopogon pratensis

GOATSBEARD

YELLOW IRIS

The Yellow Iris is an escapee from Europe and can be found throughout the entire eastern United States in wet meadows and ditches, and along shorelines and banks of streams.

This two to three-foot plant has long, sword-like leaves that stand erect along the side of the plant. The flowers have six petal-like parts. The outer three, called "falls," are really sepals, and the three inner are petals, called "standards." Most often the falls have a blotch of color called the "nectar guide," which is designed to guide the honeybee to the pollen.

Because of all these differently-shaped and colored sepals and petals, the Yellow Iris is a very striking flower. It is no wonder it has been hybridized to become popular landscape flowers. Hundreds of hybrids are available to the landscaper today in as many colors.

Many Iris have large tubers that are poisonous, but as in many cases, small quantities were used to cure illnesses.

Propagation of the Yellow Iris can sometimes be quite frustrating if you try to start it from seeds. First, the seed pods may not contain any viable seeds for several years. Seeds should be stored in a cool, dry place until spring. Starting the Yellow Iris in a greenhouse is preferred, but success is sometimes quite limited.

Best results will be obtained if the rhizomes are divided, stored in water or wet soil, and then allowed to grow in full sun. It is imperative that the roots not dry out during this process. If the rhizomes are being started in water, it is not necessary to have nutrients in the water. When a good set of roots have formed, transfer the plant to a pot of rich soil and keep moist.

Iris pseudacorus

YELLOW IRIS

TROUT LILY

The Trout Lily is indeed a true Lily. It can be found in rich forest soils throughout the United States. The Trout Lily can do well in a shaded, woodland wildflower garden, although after a few years these plants seem to die out without perfect conditions.

When blooming, this plant has two leaves that are lance-shaped and heavily mottled. Because of its mottled leaves or the way the two leaves look like a fawn's ear, it is also called the Fawn Lily. Another familiar name is Adder's Tongue, probably a result of the appearance of the long anthers, sepals, or seed head. The name Dogtooth Violet comes from the white bulbs which supposedly look like dog's teeth.

The flower is on a single stalk with three recurved, yellow sepals and three yellow petals. This spring woodland flower blooms from March through May.

The Trout Lily makes large colonies of plants, both by seeds and by its root system. For about six years the young plants have only one leaf while they store enough food in their white bulbs to produce two leaves and a flower.

As the Trout Lily is so abundant, many animals have learned to eat the leaves and roots, including man. The leaves have been used to make a tea for stomach problems. The leaves were also used as a poultice for wounds and sores.

Growing the Trout Lily from seed can be quite rewarding, but requires some careful management. The seeds mature in the pod about six weeks after blooming, or just past mid-summer. The yellowed leaves will be almost dead. The pods will be laying on the ground, so you will have to search for them.

For best results, the seeds should be collected from the pods and sown right away in a shaded, moist area of your landscape. The area should have a good layer of mulch to keep as much moisture as possible.

It will take three to four years for the Trout Lily to be viable enough to produce a flower. A quicker way to get additional plants from a prolific spot is to divide them when they have gone dormant in late summer.

Erythronium americanum

32

TROUT LILY

BUTTER-AND-EGGS

A garden plant brought over from Europe, this plant is now found wild throughout the entire eastern United States. In wildflower gardens, this plant is little used because of the beautiful varieties of Snapdragons available.

The Butter-and-eggs belongs to the Snapdragon family. The familiar flower is one-inch in length with two lips. The upper lip has two yellow lobes, while the lower has three orange lobes. This feature gives it the name 'Butter' (yellow) and 'eggs' (the orange yolks). The leaves are long, slender, grass-like and are several inches long. The arrangement of the leaves changes from whorled and opposite at the base of the two-foot plant to alternate at the top.

Butter-and-eggs is a midsummer bloomer which starts in July and is complete by October. Many times it grows in clumps because it spreads by roots as well as seeds. The blocks of yellow are very attractive along roadsides and in fallow fields or meadows.

The Europeans used this plant as a yellow dye and for its qualities as a medicinal herb. The leaves were used to make both a tea and salve because, according to the Doctrine of Signatures, it would cure throat ailments.

As the Butter-and-eggs blooms, the seed pods form at the bottom of the stalk, while the plant continues to bloom at the top. The seeds can be collected from the capsules before they mature. The capsules mature and open in the early fall when the wind scatters the wafer-shaped seeds afar. Because the seeds do not germinate until spring, they can be sown immediately or stored in a cool, dry place for the winter. The plant grows rapidly from seed and may produce flowers the first season of growth.

Probably the best way to propagate the Butter-and-eggs is to dig the rhizomes from a colony that has already formed. This will produce a nice colony of plants in a couple of years, especially if the new plants are protected from competititon. Even though the flowers of the Butter-and-eggs are visited by butterflies they do not pollinate the flowers.

Linaria vulgaris

34

BUTTER-AND-EGGS

FOXGLOVE

The Foxglove is common throughout the eastern United States and can be found in the rich soils of woodlands and forest edges. This plant is parasitic on the roots of oak trees, and so they are particularly abundant in oak forests. The Foxglove is related to the European Foxglove, of which there are many colorful ornamentals.

Indian legend gives the plant its name, saying the blossoms were put on the feet of foxes, thereby giving them gloves.

The flowers of the Foxglove, or False Foxglove, have five yellow petals which are fused into a funnel-shaped corolla. These flowers can be several inches long. This plant itself is quite tall, reaching almost six or seven feet in height. Most leaves are lance-shaped with rounded teeth, while the lower leaves can be heavily pinnately-dissected. The Foxglove blooms in late summer.

Both the Indians and the Europeans used the Foxglove medicinally to treat heart diseases, even though the Foxglove is also known to be poisonous. It is still used today for treating heart diseases.

One of the most beautiful butterflies that is common over most of the eastern United States is the Baltimore. The Baltimore butterfly makes the Foxglove its host plant for food. The Baltimore is black with spots of white and burnt orange. The trailing parts of the wings have a border of this orange color. Scattered throughout the border of black are numerous spots of cream. The underside is whiter and the orange border is significantly wider. The caterpillar is bright orange with bands of black. The segments have short stalks of black hairs. Probably the most colorful part of the Baltimore's life cycle is the chrysalis, which is predominately white with spots of black and orange scattered over the entire outer shell.

Gerardia virginica

FOXGLOVE

COMMON MULLEIN

This European biennial is easily recognized by its extremely fuzzy leaves which gives rise to many of its other names: Lamb's Ear, Velvet Plant, Flannel Plant, and Beggar's Blanket. Common Mullein is common in fields, roadsides, and waste places throughout the entire United States. The Common Mullein should be eliminated from the formal landscape, but can be used in a natural planting.

The extremely large leaves are almost white because of their covering of fuzz in the first year's basal rosette. After a season of storing food in its roots, the Common Mullein puts up a two- to six-foot stalk, atop which are found the clusters of five-petaled, yellow flowers. The leaves alternately clasp the stalk which may be branched at the top.

The Common Mullein blooms from mid-summer until frost, when it leaves behind the giant plant stalk. This candelabra-like seed source feeds Goldfinches and other winter birds with its many seeds.

The Common Mullein was also called Quaker's Rouge because Quaker ladies, who did not believe in make-up, rubbed the leaves on their cheeks to give them a rosy glow. The leaves were used to make a yellow dye, as a cure for muscle aches, as cough medicine, and as sock liners.

The velvet-feeling leaves are home to a unique insect called the Mullein Thrip. Careful observation will reveal small, pepper-shaped, black specks in the soft leaves of the basal rosette. Thrips are extremely small insects that attack plants and can become quite an economic threat in greenhouses and cultivated fields. A careful look at the Mullein Thrip will reveal that its wings are quite different from other insects in that they look like combs that have teeth on both surfaces.

Verbascum thapsus

COMMON MULLEIN

BELLWORT

The one-inch, yellow flowers of the Bellwort hang down from branched plants much like the uvula at the back of our throat. This plant has oval to oblong leaves that completely clasp the stem, making it appear as if a seamstress threaded the stem back and forth through the alternate leaves.

The Bellwort can grow about eighteen inches tall, the leaves reaching two to three inches in length. Growing in rich forested situations, this spring wildflower blooms from April through May. The Bellworts are entirely an eastern plant.

Because of the way the flower hangs on this plant it was thought to cure diseases of the throat. However, no evidence exists that supports this use. Indians used the plant to make an infusion for sore backs and other muscle ailments. Occasionally, they would mix Boneset and Bellwort together with animal fat as a method of soothing aches and pains.

The Bellworts are good perennials when used in the shady areas of our backyard landscape design. They grow fairly thickly and do nicely when mixed with ferns and lower-growing perennials.

The Bellwort is easy to grow from seeds. The seed capsules begin forming soon after the flower petals fall, forming a three-lobed seed capsule. The capsules hang down the same as the flowers did, and will be mature by the middle of the summer. The capsules should be harvested as they become mature and sown immediately in the ground. It is best to place a thin layer of sand over the top of the seeds and scratch them into the ground. You may wish to mulch the soil as the seeds begin germinating to provide adequate moisture, although they will do fairly well if left alone.

It will take a couple of years for the plants to mature and bear flowers. Transplanting the Bellwort is usually not productive. The Bellwort grows singly and removing it would be unwise.

Uvularia grandiflora

40

BELLWORT

COMMON CINQUEFOIL

Blooming from April through June, the Cinquefoil, or Five Finger as it is many times called, has five yellow petals that reach about one-half inch across. It is mostly a trailing plant and does not get very high, but it can grow over a couple of feet horizontally. The leaves are palmate with five to seven deeply-toothed leaflets, giving rise to the word "cinque" in its name, which means "five." The leaves and flowers arise from different nodes of the stem as it trails along. This variety can be found throughout the eastern United States.

Two plants that, because of their leaves, are often confused with the Cinquefoil are the Wild Strawberry and the Marijuana plant. There are many Cinquefoils, some having white or pink blossoms. They grow in dry soils in open areas. They are quite adapted to growing in poor soil.

Because of the resemblance of the Cinquefoil to the human hand, the five fingers were thought to have many healing powers. The plant was used to ward off witches as well as cure many ailments.

Many of the Copper butterflies use the Cinquefoil for their food plant. The Dorcas Copper is found over the upper midwest and New England area. This little butterfly is not as coppery in color as many of the other Coppers, but it is quite beautiful nonetheless. The Dorcas Copper is a soft, fawn-brown above, with dark brown spots in three broken lines across the wings following the outer outline. The outer brown spots are encircled with faint orange patches which really set off the spots. The underwings are much lighter and have fewer spots.

Although the Common Cinquefoil is weedy, a few varieties have been cultivated for the home landscape. The most common of these is the Potentilla fruitacosa, or Shrubby Cinquefoil. This shrub has the same five-petaled, yellow flowers as the Common Cinquefoil, and makes good borders.

Potentilla simplex

42

COMMON CINQUEFOIL

GOLDENROD

Probably no single summer or fall flower is as beautiful as the Goldenrod, and yet receives such unjustified notoriety. While the Ragweed's green flowers are blooming inconspicuously, the fields are a bright yellow with the flowers of Goldenrod. So sneezing people blame the only thing they can see–Goldenrods! Actually, the pollen of the Goldenrod is not borne by the wind, but needs insects to transport it. Ragweed pollen, the true culprit of hay fever, is distributed by the wind.

Over sixty types of Goldenrod are found throughout the eastern United States. They belong to the Daisy family, and their golden flowers are composites in showy clusters. The Goldenrods can be perennial or biennial, and usually have basal leaves that are large, becoming progressively smaller towards the top of the plant.

Goldenrods can be difficult to identify, and are divided into groups according to their growth shape. The most common are those shaped like a feather plume, flat-topped, or elm-branched. A less common shape is that of a wand, or club, growing straight up with no branching. Once the shape has been determined, you can then key the plant by its leaf arrangement, veins, and stem characteristics.

There is probably no yellow quite like the yellow of a new Goldenrod flower. They can add quite a splash of color to a natural garden. Many are easily divided and will grow in dense clumps. The flowers remain colorful for a long time, and the seeds are also quite handsome. The Goldenrods will grow in a variety of soils and light conditions depending upon the species.

Goldenrods provide a home for numerous insects, some of which cause growths called "galls" to form on the plants in which they live for a time. These galls do not seem to harm the plant. One such insect is the Susan Grub. It overwinters as a white grub which ice fishermen favor for bluegill fishing. As spring progresses, the Susan Grub pupates, and during warm weather emerges as an adult fly.

The leaves of the Goldenrod are quite aromatic when crushed. They were used for teas, a practice not recommended today. During winter, the seeds are used by birds for food.

Solidago (species)

GOLDENROD

ST. JOHNSWORT

The St. Johnswort is a common European plant of roadsides, open areas, and gardens. Its leaves are opposite, smooth, and simple. The one-inch, yellow flowers have five petals with black dots on the edges. An interesting characteristic of the St. Johnswort is the leaves, which have oblong translucent dots almost as if they were small magnifying glasses.

This flower gets its name from the fact that it blooms in England about June 24 or St. John's Day, the feastday of John the Baptist. Supposedly, the St. Johnswort holds magical powers if harvested during this time. Also, if the St. Johnswort is eaten while it is blossoming, fair-skinned animals seem to become more photosensitive, especially cattle.

Growing in most soils, the St. Johnswort can be found in old fields and fallow parts of our yards and gardens. As it is not particularly thick, this plant is not readily adapted to cultivation. About a dozen species can be found throughout the eastern United States. It grows along with the Knapweed, Ox-Eye Daisy, Queen Anne's Lace, and the Mulleins.

The pretty, yellow flowers are attractive to butterflies like the Monarch, Skipper, Sulphurs, Painted Lady, and the Red Admiral. The St. Johnswort keeps its flowers for a long time, and therefore attracts more insects for pollination. The St. Johnswort is a favorite of the soldier beetle as a host plant.

Hypericum perforatum

ST. JOHNSWORT

YELLOW ROCKET

The Yellow Rocket belongs to the Mustard family and can be found over the entire eastern United States. Its most recognizable characteristics are the four petals, which often occur in the shape of a cross or an 'X,' and the long, pencil-shaped seed pods.

Many of our cultivated garden vegetables belong in this family including cauliflower, cabbage, broccoli, kale, and turnips. The Yellow Rocket, or Winter Cress as it is often called, is not cultivated for human consumption but it is liked by cattle. Other Mustards are cultivated for their seeds which produce cooking oils such as cannola. Yellow Rocket seeds also contain great amounts of oil and provide good food for wildlife.

Yellow Rocket grows to about three feet tall, with the flowers bunched at the top of the plant. The leaves are basal and elongate. The end of the leaf has a large, egg-shaped lobe with smaller lobes down the petiole numbering about four. This plant has clasping leaves on the upper parts of the plant.

The Yellow Rocket blooms in the early spring. It provides greens from its new, basal leaves until it begins to bloom, at which time the leaves become too bitter.

Winter Cress in not used in the normal landscape plan because it is weedy in nature, and will become a problem for normal perennials. It grows in old fields, meadows, and pastures. It is a welcome sight of yellow in the early spring.

Being a Mustard, the Yellow Rocket is attractive to a number of butterflies. Both Whites and Sulphurs visit the flowers, and make the Yellow Rocket their food plant. A pretty butterfly that is found throughout the midwest is the Olympia Marblewing. It is not striking, but having just emerged from the chrysalis it is a pink, marbled color. The undersides have very soft, warm-brown streaks in the marbled white of the background. The brown streaks seem to be lined in yellow. Other Marblewings also make use of the Yellow Rocket for their food and nectar.

Barberea vulgaris

48

YELLOW ROCKET

MICHIGAN LILY

Sometimes confused with the Common Day-lily, the Michigan Lily is easily distinguished by its greatly recurved petals which are spotted. The flower also nods downward, unlike the erect Day-lily. The Michigan Lily is closer in appearance to the rare Turk's-cap Lily, as it has a green star in the center of its flower, although in the Michigan Lily the green star is not as distinct. The petals are a deep orange at the tips, shading to yellow at the throat of the flower.

Found in moist rich soil from southern Canada south to Tennessee, it is frequently transplanted to home gardens. In the wild, the Michigan Lily will grow in shady or open areas of moist wetlands. In the garden, this lily requires rich soil and must be kept from drought. The Michigan Lily will grow to about five or six feet tall, and may possibly have more than a dozen flowers throughout July and August.

Lilies, nearly from the beginning of time, have intrigued people and have given us many legends. The Tiger Lilies, of which the Michigan Lily is one, are said to have descended from a tiger that was befriended by a hermit, who removed an arrow from the tiger's leg. The tiger, upon its death, turned into a lily which spread worldwide after the hermit died because it sought its friend. Today many lilies have been hybridized to provide us with a tremendous vartiety of flowers.

These flowers are visited by the Spicebush Swallowtail butterfly, as well as the Great Spangled Fritillary. Other Swallowtails will visit this flower but not quite as readily. Not especially endowed with nectar, the Michigan Lily is not readily attractive to hummingbirds, but they do visit it because of its bright, orange color.

Lilium michiganense

MICHIGAN LILY

DAY-LILY

This three to six foot flower can be found in most of the eastern United States, except the far north and the southernmost tier of states, including Florida. The Day-lily is found along roadsides and other waste areas. The flowers of this perennial are produced on leaf-less stems. It opens daily beginning mid-summer, with the plant continually blooming for about one month.

The long, sword-like leaves arise from bulbous roots, found usually in large colonies. This orange lily as well as the less common yellow Day-lily were used extensively in plantings around homesteads, and have escaped to colonize many other areas.

All the parts of the Day-lily are said to be edible. The Europeans brought this flower with them both for its attractiveness and as a food source.

The Day-lily makes a wonderful plant around the home as it does not require much care once it is established. The plant must be started from transplanted roots because the flowers are sterile. Because of this, it is said that the Day-lilies we have in the United States probably came from one hybrid plant long ago.

Reproducing without seed, the Common Day-lily is spread by the large, tuberous roots. Sometimes this is done by man intentionally, while at other times it is done by accident. A good place to find this lily is in ditches, where it it is established when the roots are washed to different locations by water during storms, or when they are relocated by workers cleaning out the ditches. Mowing machines may also catch some and drop them further down the road. Another popular place to find these plants is at abandoned homesteads, where they were undoubtedly planted and allowed to flourish naturally.

Hemerocallis fulva

52

DAY-LILY

ORANGE HAWKWEED

When seen in a field of Ox-Eye Daisies or with other Hawkweeds, the Orange Hawkweed has to be one of the prettiest flowers of early summer. This composite has a one-inch flower of bright orange that grades to yellow orange at the center. The outer petals are squared off at the end with a ragged edge. The plant has a basal rosette of leaves, and a stalk that is very hairy.

The Orange Hawkweed can be found throughout the eastern United States down to the southern Appalachians. It prefers meadows, fields, lawns, and fallow areas in a variety of soils. This European weed grows about eighteen to twenty-four inches tall, and prefers open sunlight.

The name of Hawkweed came about because of a story that the plant would give you the eyesight of a hawk if eaten. Another name for this plant is Devil's Paintbrush due to the bright, orange colors found on the devil's brush.

As in the other Hawkweeds, this plant is not considered for horticultural gardens, although it can add color to an otherwise drab area. The seeds are dispersed, much like Dandelions, on tiny parachutes. The basal rosette of leaves can take on a variety of colors which make an attractive ground cover.

Although the food plant of the Pearly Crescent butterfly is the Aster, one of the nectar plants preferred is the Orange Hawkweed. Along with the Hawkweed, it also prefers other members of the Daisy family: Milkweed, Clovers, and Peppermints.

The Indians of the Great Lakes region used the Hawkweed as a spiritual omen to ward off the Manitous that would hurt the summer berry crops by picking the flowers and placing them with fish bones to ensure a good harvest.

Hieracium aurantiacum

54

ORANGE HAWKWEED

JEWELWEED

This flower grows along streams, marshes, in ditches, and in other wet areas. It prefers to have some shade where it will grow to about five or six feet. The one-inch flowers are orange with darker orange or brown spots. The flower is comprised of a spurred sack made from the sepals, with three petals forming the front of the flowers. The leaves are oblong with smooth-edged teeth. The stem is succulent and somewhat translucent. A late germinate, the flowers come out in the mid-summer and may last until September. It is common in its habitat over the eastern United States.

The name Jewelweed is quite appropriate as the leaves repel the water of dew or rain, forming little beads. In the early morning sun, these little drops appear to be jewels. The plant is also called Touch-Me-Not, or Snapweed, because of its seed pods. They are about one inch in length and are shaped like a banana. As they mature, the inner pod dries unevenly so tension is placed on the hull. If touched, the hull snaps and splits into five or so strips which coil up rapidly, thereby flinging the seeds inside everywhere.

At two times during the year, the Jewelweed is extremely visible and easy to identify. The easiest is in the summer and fall, when the orange flowers are blooming and the plant is nearly three feet tall. The other is in the spring as the soil begins to warm and the new seeds from last year's Touch Me Not have seeded themselves, and produced two roundish leaves about the size of a penny. The ground is usually littered with them, as they begin to grow before most plants have had a chance to start. In a few days they will shoot up another batch of leaves looking more like the adult plant's leaves with rounded teeth.

The plant stems are quite succulent. The juice of the plant when rubbed on rashes such as those caused by Poison Ivy, can cure, or at least alleviate, the itching. The young stems have been eaten raw as a spring herb.

Impatiens capensis

JEWELWEED

BUTTERFLY-WEED

Bright orange is the only way to describe the color of this member of the Milkweed family. Except for the northern part of Maine and extreme southern Florida where it is not found, the Butterfly-weed is almost exclusively an eastern plant.

This perennial differs from the other Milkweeds in three obvious ways: the flowers are orange; the leaves are alternate; and the sap is clear, not milky. The leaves are similar, although narrower, to the Common Milkweed, being lance-shaped and about five inches long. The plant is hairy, giving it a grayish cast. The orange flowers are born in clusters at the top of the plant and have the typical recurved horns from the corolla. The seed pods are similar to the Common Milkweed, being thinner but nearly the same length.

As its name indicates, the Butterfly-weed does indeed attract copious amounts of butterflies and other insects. It is an easy plant to establish in a perennial garden, and readily available as roots or potted plants at most good garden centers or nurseries.

Another common name for the Butterfly-weed was the Pleurisy Root from the belief that a potion made from the root would cure pleurisy. A brew of the seed pods or leaves was also used for other maladies. The young pods and spring shoots were used as cooked greens, much like the Common Milkweed, although not preferred over the Common Milkweed.

Besides the Monarch Butterfly, the Queen Butterfly likes the Milkweed family for its food plant. The Queen is actually a very pretty butterfly that is burnt orange in color with black edging on the wings. It has scattered white spots in the black edge and some in the forward wing's outermost points. Unfortunately, this butterfly is not as widespread as the Monarch, limited to the south. You may introduce it in the north for the summer's enjoyment, but it will not over-winter.

Asclepias tuberosa

58

BUTTERFLY-WEED

TRUMPET CREEPER

As the name indicates, this bright orange flower is trumpet-shaped and about three inches long. It has five lobes to the corolla. The leaves are pinnately compound, with five to eleven toothed leaflets. As the word "creeper" in the name indicates, this flower acts like a vine, but is not as ambitious as the Bindweed or Morning Glory. The Trumpet Creeper can get quite old and grow, with support, tens of feet high. Vines over six inches in diameter growing over twenty feet tall upon a pole are not uncommon.

Found throughout the eastern United States, the Trumpet Creeper is sought after for its pretty, orange flower. In the wild it can be a nuisance, making a tangle of vines that are hard to remove. Old farmers used to call this plant the Hell Vine and shook their head when people actually purchased these plants from a nursery.

Blooming during the summer, this flower is extremely pretty, and can be a welcome addition to a hedge or trellis. Hummingbirds and moths are extremely attracted to this plant. With a little care you can have a well-trained vine that attracts hummingbirds all summer long. Horticulturists have developed several color variations. The pencil-long seed pods can be harvested in the fall and planted.

Children also use the flowers of the Trumpet Creeper as dolls with orange dresses. This is also done with Hollyhock flowers.

Campsis radicans

TRUMPET CREEPER

SOLOMON'S-SEAL

Unlike the False Solomon's-seal, the true Solomon's-seal has green flowers hanging down in pairs from the alternate leaf axis. Other than this, the plants are so similar they may be difficult to separate during the times of no berries or blooms. Both plants may reach two to three feet in height. The leaves are broadly lance-shaped. The green flowers turn into blue, grape-like berries during the last part of summer and early fall.

The Solomon's-seal prefers rich forests and swamp lands. A flower of the understory of the forest, the Solomon's-seal blooms in the spring through early summer. Unlike many woodland flowers, Solomon's-seal does not die back during the summer.

Some debate exists as to where the name of this plant originated. Some say it came from the fact that the roots were used to seal the wounds of soldiers. Or it may be because the roots have a scar from the growth of the previous year's rhizome, which some say appears to be that of a royal seal.

The young, fresh shoots of the Solomon's-seal are edible cooked as you would asparagus. The roots were ground up and used as salve to take out the swelling and black-and-blue marks of bruises. The roots were also eaten as a cooked vegetable. A tea was used from the leaves as a contraceptive.

Solomon's-seal, and others of the species, make wonderful garden plants when used to accent a shady, perennial bed. Horticulture experts have hybridized it to provide variations in the leaves, height, and flowers. The Solomon's-seal prefers slightly acidic soils.

The Solomon's-seal is a plant of the deep shade, but must have rich soil. This plant is is best used for its green foliage, and the curving, graceful arc of the plant. Coupled with some ferns and a few False Solomon's-seal, the effect is quite striking. Occasionally, you may wish to use the long, graceful plants at the edge of a perennial garden, hanging over a border of small, blooming flowers.

Polygonatum biflorum

SOLOMON'S SEAL

LAMB'S-QUARTER

This weed has been included because it is so common in the backyard garden. The Lamb's-quarter is an annual weed that we have inherited from Europe. It loves to grow in disturbed soils, such as flower or vegetable gardens. The overall shape of the alternate leaf is elliptical, but because it has sort of a triangle at the base it looks like its namesake, the hindquarter of a lamb, when dressed out at the butcher shop.

This weed grows and blooms quickly as the soil warms with summer, blooming from June until frost. The flowers are not noticeable as they are small and green. The seeds also are very inconspicuous, even though the plant may reach six feet in height. Because of the height of the Lamb's-quarter, it provides a good food source for wintering birds, as it does not get covered by snow, except during extreme conditions.

Other plants in this group are chard, spinach, and beets. The leaves of this plant have been used as cooked greens during the early part of the season when they are more tender and less bitter. Late in the season the leaves, flowers, and seeds may become tinged with red. Being an annual, this plant must grow new each season from seed.

The seeds of Lamb's-quarter remain viable for hundreds of years in the soil waiting to germinate when and if the right conditions come along. What the Lamb's-quarter needs is warm soil and some moisture. The Lamb's-quarter is a typical weed, in that the plant will grow quite rapidly and produce a flower in as little as two to three weeks. This makes it especially obnoxious to the vegetable gardener who must be on the watch for these weeds weekly, if not daily. One thing the seed cannot stand is dry soil, so a thin layer of loose soil at the surface will keep the Lamb's-quarter under check.

Chenopodium album

64

LAMB'S-QUARTER

JACK-IN-THE-PULPIT

Anyone who has spent time in the spring forest knows the Jack-in-the-Pulpit. The flower is very distinct, being a tube with a canopy bending over the top. The flower is green with differently-colored stripes running up the flower into the hood. The most common color is purple, but varying shades of green are also interspersed. These colors make this plant very beautiful.

The Jack-in-the-Pulpit has either one or two leaves, each having three leaflets like the Trillium. The flower grows almost three inches high, with the entire plant growing almost three feet in height. The Jack-in-the-Pulpit prefers rich soils that retain a fair amount of moisture in the humus. As the summer progresses, the plant dies back, leaving the berries to mature to a bright, red cluster.

Interestingly, the flowers of the Jack-in-the-Pulpit are separate in sex. Evidently it takes the plant a while to store enough energy in the tuber to make a flower, sometimes taking three or more years. Once the flower is grown, the plant usually has but one leaf and the flower is probably male. After a few more years of growing, the tuber may become large enough to produce a second set of leaves, and the flower will become a female. Occasionally, both sexes may be present on the same plant. If the plant has been stressed, the next season's growth will only allow a single leaf and the flower will revert back to a male, until enough energy is built up in the tuber once again.

This plant has also been called Indian Turnip, probably by farm children out to play a cruel hoax on their unsuspecting city cousins. The plant is filled with crystals of calcium oxalate which gives a severe burning sensation to the mucus membrane. The plant is inedible, and is even said to be poisonous. Settlers and Indians used the plant for a poultice for wounds.

The Jack-in-the-Pulpit is a wonderful plant to add to a shade garden. It blooms in late spring for a long duration, and requires little care except rich soil and a fair amount of moisture. The rich, red clusters of berries add a dimension to the forest floor in the fall that is a welcome sight. These berries can be harvested and planted in new garden locations.

Arisaema triphyllum

JACK-IN-THE-PULPIT

COMMON RAGWEED

Although heavily maligned as the cause for the sneezing and suffering of hay fever victims, the Common Ragweed is not easily recognized as the culprit because of its inconspicuous flowers. Both the Common Ragweed and Great Ragweed have small, green flowers that produce the wind-dispersed pollen that irritates so many. The pollen is dispersed by the wind because the flowers do not attract a significant number of insects. The leaves can be opposite or alternate, and are finely divided into pointed lobes.

The Common Ragweed can grow several feet tall, whereas the Great Ragweed can grow over ten feet tall. The leaves of the Great Ragweed are larger and less dissected. Both Ragweeds are native to, and can be found, throughout the United States in disturbed soils.

The Ragweeds are considered a weedy plant. In attempting to define the term "weed," most experts name those plants that are adapted to the disturbance of soil. This is why we find so many 'weeds' in our gardens. After we disk or till the soil, the seeds that are in the soil grow rapidly, and if we do not keep up with weeding, these plants will overtake our garden.

A good feature of the Common Ragweed is the types of butterflies to which it is host. A pretty butterfly that eats the Common Ragweed is the Gorgone Crescentspot. This butterly is a colorful black and orange, somewhat reminiscent of the Monarch. The favorite nectar flower of the Crescentspot is the Sunflower. Another butterfly that eats the Ragweed is the Bordered Patch. This butterfly is predominately black with a broad band of orange abut halfway through the wings.

Ambrosia artemisiifolia

COMMON RAGWEED

GINGER

The Wild Ginger is not the ginger we think of as a spice for our gingerbread houses. However, its root has been used as a substitute for the true Ginger root.

The Wild Ginger has a heart-shaped leaf that can reach over six inches across as summer progresses. The entire plant is hairy. Two leaves arise from root stems, and from these comes a brown to maroon-colored, cup-shaped flower with three calyx lobes coming to a point. This flower lies close to the ground under the leaves, and is not often seen even by those who are familiar with the plant. The flowers bloom from April to May.

The points of the calyx are longer in the Smoky Mountain variety of Wild Ginger than the northern variety. Wild Ginger is found in the eastern United States, and as far south as the Carolinas.

Along with using the root as a true Ginger substitute, the plant was used in a tea to cure a variety of sicknesses including whooping cough, and the leaves were used to treat wounds. It has since been found that some antibiotic qualities are indeed found in its leaves.

In the spring, many plants produce flowers which are neither beautiful nor which smell very good. These flowers and plants attract a host of insects other than butterflies and bees, usually beetles and flies. Flowers need to be fertilized, and they must attract whichever insect is available. Since many flies and beetles overwinter as adults, they are available immediately for cross-fertilization. The flies and beetles are attracted to the carrion of animals that have died during the winter. Therefore, some flowers, like the Wild Ginger, imitate that carrion smell, making them attractive to flies and beetles. Recent research indicates they also do some self-pollination.

Wild Ginger is a very hardy plant to use in a shade ground cover. The leaves will make a full bed of beautiful heart-shaped green. Because of the demand for this plant for perennial gardens, most nurseries handle them in pots.

Asarum canadense

GINGER

COMMON BLUE VIOLET

Sometimes called the Meadow Violet, the Common Blue Violet is found throughout the entire eastern United States. It can be found in a variety of habitats, including woodlands, lawns, waysides, meadows, and hillside ledges. This violet has five petals, two facing upward and three facing downward, with the center of the three having a white marking at its base. This center petal also extends behind the flower to provide a small spur. The flowers and leaves are on separate stalks.

The Common Blue Violet has a second set of flowers which do not grow very tall and do not open, but produce great quantities of seeds which greatly enhances the ability of this perennial to reproduce. The taller, more visible, flowers are picked, either by people or wildlife, as they are a delicacy, leaving the short flowers to perpetuate the species.

The seeds are dispersed when the seed pod dries out and explodes the seeds as far as ten to twelve feet from the plant. Such mechanical dispersion may explain why this Violet spreads so quickly. Common Blue Violet is easy to transplant to yards, and even though it spreads rapidly it is not offensive as it does not crowd out other species of garden plants.

The Violet will attract many butterflies, among them the Fritillaries and Spring Azure. The Violet provides nectar to butterflies, while caterpillars feed on the leaves. The Great Spangled Fritillary visits many plants in the open meadows and marshes, but its larval food is the Violet. This light orange butterfly with black spots is not all that striking until it flies or shows its underwing. Then the bright silver spots show, making this butterfly the outstanding prize it is.

Violets have long been used as spring greens and green garnishment to salads. The blossoms have been use to add color to drinks and salads. The flowers have even been made into jellies and candies.

Viola papilionacea

COMMON BLUE VIOLET

BLUE FLAG IRIS

The Blue Flag Iris is a common flower of wet soils. Two similar species, size being the only major difference, exist in wetlands ranging throughout the eastern United States and Canada, from Maine to near the southern end of the Appalachian Mountains.

These flowers are made up of petals and sepals, with the sepals being wider and more showy. The sepals have a yellow center vein called a "nectar guide." This blotch of yellow is thought to lead butterflies and bees to the center of the flower for cross-pollination. The leaves are long and slender with parallel veins. The plant reaches a height of about three feet.

There are many theories about the origin of the name Blue Flag, ranging from their use as cemetery plantings which bloomed prolifically on Flag Day, to the idea that they appear "flag-like" and so are called "flags."

The Blue Flag Iris requires rich, moist soils and can easily be grown in a perennial flower bed with some care. Although it does best in full sun, the Blue Flag Iris can also grow well in partial shade, and even provides a good undergrowth bloom in an open, wooded situation. This plant blossoms from mid-May through mid-summer, with individual flowers remaining for relatively long periods.

The Blue Flag Iris grows by rhizomes. It also produces seeds which fall to the ground in the fall, or the following spring, and germinate. The first couple of years, the new plants only produce leaves, but by the third year it should be strong enough to produce a flower. Iris colonies that grow at the edge of water seem to be limited by the depth of the water and competition from land-borne plants.

Iris versicolor

74

BLUE FLAG IRIS

NEW ENGLAND ASTER

Asters belong to the composite family. They have many male and female flowers in a central head, with large, female flowers surrounding them. These large, outer, female flowers are called "ray flowers." They give the flower a star-like appearance to which the word "aster" refers. The asters are bushy plants with alternate leaves.

The New England Aster has leaves that are lance-shaped, without teeth, and clasp the stem. The leaves are more abundant and bunched together than other asters. The New England Aster may grow to a height of over six feet, and the flowers may be as much as two inches wide. The attractiveness of this Aster lies in its dark, purple-violet color. A field of New England Aster in full bloom in the fall is a sight to behold. Luckily it grows freely in abandoned fields, meadows, marshes, and roadsides throughout the eastern United States.

Because this plant is so attractive and eye-catching in the fall, it is sought after to compliment many landscapes. Cultivated New England Aster is often called Michaelmas Daisy.

Since it is one of the last flowers to bloom, along with the Fall White Aster, it is popular with many insects and bees. During the winter, birds will make use of the seeds, as the plant is tall and stiff enough to remain above most heavy snows.

Considered a frost aster, the New England Aster blooms as the days become cooler and shorter. During the summer it stores energy for the fall production of flowers and the next growing season. Once the days become shorter and the temperatures drop, this flower will begin to set buds and bloom. Some say that the fall blooming season takes advantage of the great number of insects that mature in the summer. It is believed that the cool nights help give the New England Aster its deep blue color.

Aster novae-angliae

NEW ENGLAND ASTER

HAREBELL

The Harebell has a blue flower with five petals fused into a corolla. The flower is nearly one inch long. The leaves are simple, wiry, and alternate, with heart-shaped basal leaves. The plant rarely grows to two feet. In the eastern United States, the Harebell is only found as far south as Kentucky.

In Scotland and England, the Harebell is called the Bluebell. The flower is indeed a "blue bell" and only a little imagination is required to conjure tinkling sounds coming from the bright, blue flowers. The Harebell grows in meadows, grassy fields, edges, and even into the mountains. It blooms from mid-summer into the fall.

Because of the capacity of this flower to withstand harsh winds and temperatures, it is a prized plant in the gardens of Scotland and England. Today we have hybridized it and a number of similar plants are available from the same family for our perennial beds.

The Harebell flower matures at different times for the different sexual appendages. The male portion produces pollen first, and then the stigma will accept pollen later from insects. If the plant does not become fertilized, the pistil will bend down into the collected pollen from the earlier maturing stamens. This feature ensures that cross-fertiziliation will have the best chance to occur, with the last resort being that the plant will at least be able to produce seeds.

The Brown Elfin and Common Blue butterflies will take nectar from the Harebell, but their food plants are shrubs, lupines, and milkweed. Bumblebees are successful in getting nectar from the Harebell, but they do not prefer them because the amount of nectar is not great.

Campanula rotundifolia

HAREBELL

DAYFLOWER

Related to the Spiderwort, the Dayflower only blooms once a day in the morning. The flower is composed of three petals, two of which are large, blue, and above the smaller, white one. The flowers are seemingly held up by a modified heart-shaped leaf cupping the stem. Actually all the leaves clasp the stem. The leaves are smooth, lance-shaped, and pointed on the end.

This plant can grow to three feet long, but its habit of creeping across the ground with only the flowered portion raising up makes it appear shorter. The Dayflower prefers rich soil near forest edges with some shading, and is primarily an eastern plant, not yet found in the west. The Dayflower is an annual, grows quite rapidly from seeds, and can be used to fill in where a nice ground cover is needed. It can also become a nuisance where not wanted.

The Dayflower is an easy plant to grow. All that is needed is a glass of water in which to place a cutting where it will root. It is often used in planters because it grows so rapidly and thickly. Some types of Dayflowers have been hybridized to produce foliage that is striking in itself, and can be enticed to grow quite large.

When starting a new landscape area, the Dayflower is an excellent choice as it will grow quickly, and fills the area with pretty foliage and flowers. Once a decision has been made about which other flowers will be used in the landscape, the Dayflower will pull out easily with little resistance.

The Indians used this plant for a potherb, and boiled the roots for a potato substitute. The leaves were eaten by older people to increase sexual potency.

Commelina communis

80

DAYFLOWER

BLUE VERVAIN

The flowers of the Blue Vervain are very small, usually less than one-quarter inch in width. They are five-petaled, and are fused together. What makes the plant so interesting is the spikes upon which the flowers grow. Some have likened them to candelebras or the skinny fingers of a hand. The blue-violet flowers bloom from the bottom of the spike, encircling it and then moving upward. Old timers say that when the flowers reach the top it will frost. The leaves are lance-shaped with sharp-pointed teeth. The stem is somewhat four-sided or squarish, and the entire plant can grow to nearly six feet tall.

The Vervains prefer wet soils and can be found in ditches, marshes, swamps, and stream sides. It is common throughout the eastern United States, but less abundant in the extreme southern states.

The Verbena family, to which the Blue Vervain belongs, is very attractive to hummingbirds and butterflies. Many cultivators have been produced for the garden because of the extraordinary ability of the flower to attract hummingbirds. However, neither the blue or white varieties of Vervain are particularly attractive in the home landscape.

Some have said that the Blue Vervain has aphrodisiacal qualities, and others that it is spiritual or magical. It is not certain whether the Vervain gets its supposed mystical powers from the finger-shaped flowers, or for some other unknown reason.

The Blue Vervain is visited by many butterflies during the blooming season. A few of the butterfly larvae will use the Blue Vervain as a food plant, especially when it grows early in the season. The Skippers and Swallowtails like the flowers of this plant, probably because it grows in close proximity to other wetland species they prefer.

Verbena hastata

BLUE VERVAIN

HEAL-ALL

Heal-all, or Selfheal as it is often called, is a Mint. It carries opposite leaves, square-shaped stems, and two-lipped and orchid-shaped flowers that arise from the leaf axils, or at the terminis. Most of the Mints are aromatic, and some are pleasantly scented.

Heal-all grows six to twelve inches tall and was brought here from Europe to provide a cure to many illnesses. Through the years it has been used as a throat medicine and a wound dressing. It can be found all over the United States today and blooms from May to the end of the summer. The flowers are blue to violet, and may even have some white on them. As in most of the Mints, the flowers are quite pretty when looked at closely. Heal-all grows in a variety of soils but does best in rich humus.

When grown in a garden setting, the Mints can be quite attractive when used as a ground cover. Heal-all, as well as Purple Dead-nettle, are being used in landscape design today as alternatives to some traditional plants such as Pachysandra.

Heal-all is popular with some butterflies, most of which are small and inconspicuous. A butterfly that will take nectar from the Heal-all is the Swallowtail. Most of the Swallowtails prefer the leaves of shrubs and trees for their food plants, but will visit a number of plants for nectar. The Swallowtails are a large butterfly with long tails trailing from the rear of the underwing. Most of them are colored yellow with black or black with yellow. At the base of the tail on the underwing very colorful spots can usually be found, sometimes appearing as eyes. A couple of the Swallowtails taste bad and so are avoided by predators. Other butterflies imitate these distasteful Swallowtails to protect themselves. Another butterfly that prefers the Heal-all is the American Painted Lady.

Prunella vulgaris

HEAL-ALL

CHICORY

Chicory was used as a coffee substitute for centuries in European cultures during times when coffee was scarce and extremely costly. The long taproot is roasted and used in place of or as an additive. Some prefer to add the roasted root to give more flavor and body at less cost. The root has also been used, without much popularity, as a cooked vegetable and the leaves as greens.

This plant can grow to a height of four feet. The flowers are small, usually less than one inch across. The blue petals are squared at the end with a jagged edge. The leaves are similar to that of the Dandelion, being double-toothed, and they appear as a basel rosette. The leaves become smaller as they go up the plant, and they clasp the stem.

Chicory blooms from mid-summer until frost. The best time to see Chicory is in the morning as the flowers are gone or wasted by mid-afternoon. The blue flowers are especially fond of roadsides, but can also be found in many fallow fields and waste places throughout the entire United States. Chicory can be quite attractive in a natural meadow setting, but as a wild-flower in a formal setting it is not dense enough.

Some of the Plains Indians and Indians of the desert southwest would grind the roasted root of the Chicory and mix it with the plants of some of the hallucino-genic cactus and herbs of the plains. This mixture was also said to have been smoked and traded by and between some of the northern tribes. Some of the early settlers used the new, green leaves of this plant as a spring tonic although not much is known about the medicinal values of the Chicory. More than likely the plant has about as much value as any spring green such as the Plantain or Dandelion. After a long winter a fresh new plant is a welcome sight no matter what the taste or benefit.

Goldfinches and other song-birds eat the seeds produced by the Chicory and will feed exten-sively until the seeds are gone.

Cichorium intybus

CHICORY

LUPINE

The Wild Lupine has blue pea-like flowers that are on a tall raceme at the top of the plant. The leaves are palmately divided into seven to nine leaflets. The plants may reach two feet tall. The Lupine grows in the dry soils of open woods and meadows. The blue variety of Lupine is the species common over the eastern United States.

This plant grows a very large taproot which allows the plant to survive a drought and produce a large flower head. Because of the taproot it is difficult to transplant. The plants start readily from seeds, but the most successful way is to buy the plant from your local garden center. This plant makes a very nice bed of flowers and leaves. The ornamental varieties get much larger with a greater variety of color.

The Texas Bluebonnet is a Lupine. Many dwarf species of Lupine exist in the mountains and tundra. Besides the beautiful flowers, the leaves hold a special attraction when it rains. The center of the whorl of leaves holds a drop of water which looks like a bright jewel. The Dwarf Lupine found on the Pribilof Island of St. Paul has a special name for this jewel, the St. Paul Sapphire.

Lupines are plants of the prairie and open spaces which are frequented by numerous butterflies. Two butterflies that use the Lupine as a favorite food plant and nectar source are the Eastern Tailed Blue and the Melissa Blue. In some states, the Karner Blue may be eligible for the endangered or threatened species lists. Using the Lupine in the backyard landscape may help this butterfly remain a viable species.

Lupinus perennis

LUPINE

SPIDERWORT

Used throughout the United States as a garden flower, the Spiderwort is not found in the wild. Spiderwort makes a great border plant with a mat of leaves and pretty flowers that bloom during late spring and summer. The Spiderwort prefers rich soils at forest edges and in wet meadows.

The flowers of Spiderwort open in the morning and die back later in the day, turning into gooey fluid. The stems are also prone to give off a sticky, runny fluid when broken. Because of these characteristics the Spiderwort has also been called Snotgrass and Widow's Tears.

The one-inch flowers are set above two leaf-like bracts in a cluster. The flowers may be blue, violet, or pink in color and have three petals that are somewhat triangular in shape with prominent yellow stamens. The leaves are long and grass-like, reaching over a foot in length, with the entire plant reaching over two feet in height.

Because of the desirability of this plant in the backyard setting, a number of methods are used to propagate this species. The easiest method is to allow the stems to lay upon the ground and root from the leaf node. After it is well-rooted, the stems may be cut close to the original plant and transplanted. Since this plant tends to clump, it may also be divided by taking plugs from dense portions of the group and transplanting them. Transplanting should be done in the fall or very early spring.

Capturing the seeds is also a viable way to cultivate this plant. Once the seeds have set, the stalks can be placed in a jar of water and left to mature. This is usually more successful than trying to collect them as they ripen and fall from the seed pods. The seeds need to go into dormancy for a few months before planting. This can be done by placing them in a refrigerator or by just leaving them outside for the winter. Seeding is probably the least desirable way to grow this plant.

Tradescantia virginiana

SPIDERWORT

TEASEL

This biennial grows to between three to six feet tall and remains erect for several years. The heavily-spined flower head is about two inches in length and is shaped like an egg. The lavender or lilac-colored flowers begin blooming in the center of the head, encircling it. The flowers then progressively bloom upward and downward, eventually forming two lines encircling the plant. The flowers are small and tubular with four irregular petals. The leaves are lance-shaped and clasp the stem.

The entire plant is extremely spiny, and anyone who handles it must wear heavy gloves. The spiny flower heads were first used to card or tease the nap of wool, hence the names Gypsy Comb and Teasel.

With the advent of modern technology, the only persistent use of the Teasel is in dried flower arrangements. Hundreds of Teasel stalks are harvested every fall and dyed to complement fall bouquets.

Teasel can easily be grown in the garden However, it spreads quickly and can become a nuisance. Teasel can be found in old fields in the company of summer wildflowers like the Evening Primrose, Queen Anne's Lace, Goldenrod, and Asters. Sometimes the Teasel can be found in moist ditches with the Joe-Pye-Weed, Ironweed, Boneset, and the Sunflower. An escapee from Europe, it has adapted to many different habitats where it can produce large colonies of plants numbering in the thousands in just a few short years.

Since the leaves cup the stem, they capture rainwater. Long ago this rainwater was believed to be capable of quenching even the most powerful thirst of travelers. It was also reputed to be able to get rid of warts, and was used as a sterile eye wash as well.

Dipsacus sylvestris

TEASEL

PURPLE DEAD-NETTLE

Another Mint, the Purple Dead-nettle exhibits the typical characteristics of the Mint family. As well as the square stem, opposite leaves, and aromatic leaves, it has orchid-like flowers. The flowers are long and tubular, with a lower lip that is divided into three lobes. The upper lobe is split into two lobes.

The petals of the flowers are usually pink or lavender in color, and many times they are spotted. The flowers arise from the leaf axils on the Purple Dead-nettle, but may be exhibited as spikes on the terminis of the plant as in other Mints. The flower of the Purple Dead-nettle blooms in the spring and continues throughout summer and fall.

The Purple Dead-nettle can be found growing throughout the entire United States in a variety of conditions ranging from forest edges to fields. It grows to about one foot in height, and the tube-like flowers are about one-half inch long. The leaves are heart-shaped with short, rounded teeth. The upper leaves are purplish in color, giving the impression from a distance that they are also a flower.

The Purple Dead-nettle is more shade tolerant than the other Mints. It does not smell as good as other Mints, but it does have a decided odor.

The Purple Dead-nettle usually makes a mat of plants, numbering from a dozen to over a hundred. It can be quite attractive. Landscape designers have hybridized this plant to use as a ground cover around houses.

Lamium purpureum

PURPLE DEAD-NETTLE

PURPLE VETCH

The Purple Vetch, or American Vetch as it is sometimes called, is common all over the eastern United States in roadsides, meadows, cultivated fields, hedgerows, and old fields. It blooms from May through mid-summer.

This vine is a legume belonging to the Pea family, which means it adds nitrogen to the soil. It does this with nitrogen-fixing bacteria that live on the roots in structures called "nodules." This plant is used many times for soil enhancement by growing it and then tilling it back into the soil.

The vine can grow several feet long, and has pinnately-compound leaves with tendrils at the ends. These tendrils twist around objects to allow the plant to climb and hang. The flowers are one-half inch long and tubular, with the ends being pea-like. The flowers give way to long, slender, black pods resembling thin beans which dry and twist open, releasing the seeds inside. These seeds are small, round, black, and pea-like.

The Purple Vetch, as originally brought to the United States, was a forage crop for farm animals. It eventually escaped to the wild and is quite common today. With hybridization of different alfalfa plants and grasses, the Vetch is no longer popular as a forage plant.

Quite a few species of butterflies make Purple Vetch their favorite plant. One of the most common and most abundant is the Common Sulphur. This yellow butterfly has black wing edges, with some black spots in the forewing and orange spots on the hindwing. The underwings are quite striking, being a light green with pretty eye spots. The Orange Sulphur may also use the Vetch for a food plant, and is similar in color except it is orange where the Common Sulphur is yellow. Two other butterflies in the same group of Sulphurs are the Sleepy Orange and the Fairy Yellow. These two butterflies are not as widespread as the Common Sulphur, being limited to the southern United States.

Vicia americana

PURPLE VETCH

MORNING GLORY

The Morning Glory has a large, two-inch flower, shaped like a bell or trumpet. It is quite variable in color, the most common being purple, but pink and blue are also possible. The Morning Glory is a vine and it twines around any object very successfully, sometimes to the detriment, or even the demise, of the host plant.

The flowers are five-parted, a feature which is evident even if they are fused together, by the flower pleats. The leaves are heart-shaped and smooth, sometimes measuring a few inches in width.

Growing profusely in the south, the Morning Glory is found in rich soils over the entire eastern United States. The seeds are hard. Birds sometimes eat them with little benefit as they pass through unscathed, only to start a new plant beneath some wire or tree limb. In planting your own seeds, it may be helpful to scarify or scratch the outer shell in order to weaken it and facilitate germination.

Blooming in the morning, the flowers attract many moths and hummingbirds. By mid-day the flowers have folded up into the five folds. The flowers bloom from summer to fall. Being a vine, their length may be as long as fifteen feet. Providing a trellis as a frame for the vines to grow on will give you a natural screen or border.

Today, due to hybridization, numerous colors are available to gardeners in their quest to attract butterflies and hummingbirds. Studies show that flowers which are bright red, orange, or purple, are extremely attractive to butterflies and hummingbirds. Couple this with long, tubular flowers which keep away the smaller insects, and you have just what the hummingbirds want.

The Morning Glory fits this description perfectly. Even the native colors of Morning Glory are extremely attractive to hummingbirds, but the hybrids even more so.

Ipomoea purpurea

MORNING GLORY

DEADLY NIGHTSHADE

For a long time, tomatoes were thought to be poisonous because they belonged to the same family as the Deadly Nightshade, the *Solanaceae*. This family also includes the familiar potatoes, eggplants, and peppers. Sometimes called Bittersweet Nightshade, the Deadly Nightshade is indeed poisonous.

Plants in this group can be foreboding, sprouting spines, but can also be quite attractive, as is the case in the Deadly Nightshade. The flowers are a regal purple, with curved-back petals and a protruding yellow center that is star-like. The leaves are oval with two basal leaves or lobes.

The flowers give way to small, egg-shaped berries that become bright red. Unfortunately, the berries are both poisonous and very attractive to small children. Indeed, all parts of this plant are poisonous. However, the Deadly Nightshade family has numerous plants where the fruit is edible and quite palatable, while on the same plant the stems and leaves are not.

The Deadly Nightshade is found throughout the United States in the rich soils of woodlands, brushy edges, and marshes. It can also be found growing in our yards, the seeds probably dropped by wildlife. Because of its poisonous nature it is best to eradicate this plant.

When considering plants which are poisonous to humans, we automatically assume they are poisonous to animals and insects as well. However, this is not necessarily true. For instance, the Deadly Nightshade is the food plant to a group of moths that belong to the Hawk Moth family. The larval stages of these moths actually thrive on this family of plants which have poisonous berries.

Sometimes the larval stages use the host plant's poison, or at least its distaste, to their advantage as does the Monarch and some of the Swallowtail butterflies. Adapting to a group of plants that no one else is able to utilize minimizes competition.

Solanum dulcamara

DEADLY NIGHTSHADE

IRONWEED

The Ironweed belongs to the Daisy family, and so has a compound flower head. The flowers are violet to purple in color, about one-third of one inch across, and are openly clustered at the top of the plant.

Ironweed begins blooming in August and is finished by October. The six-foot plants are found throughout the eastern United States in moist areas along streams, lakes, and in wetlands. The toothed leaves are lance-shaped and nearly ten inches in length. The undersides of the leaves are hairy, giving them a downy look.

The name Ironweed may have originated because of its hard stem. Another reason may be the rust-red seeds that form after the flower has quit blooming.

Nothing is prettier than a late-summer marsh featuring the purple of the Ironweed, the pinks of the Joe-Pye-Weed and Swamp Milkweed, the white of Boneset, and the yellow of the Sunflower. Coupled with the colorful beauty of butterflies, the late-summer marsh can be unforgettable.

This perennial can also be found in pastures where cattle will not eat it, but graze around it.

These tall plants remain above all but the deepest snows and provide seeds for winter birds. They are sometimes used in dried flower arrangements.

The Ironweed is the food plant for the American Painted Lady butterfly which feeds upon the leaves and new flowers. The caterpillar is easy to identify because it has spiny hairs across its back, arising from large black spots that have smaller pink and white spots within the black. The Painted Lady overwinters as a chrysalis. If you look closely on the tall, overwintering plants you may find one. Other butterflies that prefer the flowers of the Ironweed are Tiger Swallowtail, Skippers, Monarch, and the Fritillaries.

The Ironweed is used in natural plantings where prairie and wetland species are needed. A tall backdrop of these plants can be quite impressive.

Vernonia altissima

102

IRONWEED

HEPATICA

The Doctrine of Signatures gives this plant its more common name, Liver Leaf. In olden times, people believed that this plant held medicinal value because of the shape that it took from the human body. The three lobes of the leaves of the Hepatica resemble those of the human liver, hence the name Liver Leaf.

The Hepatica is a spring flower of the forest. It blooms early, beginning in March and except for the far north is completed by mid-May. This flower can be found throughout the eastern United States. The blooms raise up on hairy stems above last year's leaves, and produce one-inch flowers that have six to ten petals.

The color of the flower petals can vary greatly from plant to plant. Some plants will have deep violet flowers shading to various hues of blue. Other flowers may have pink flowers that grade to complete white. The old leaves are quite pretty in their own right being shades of green, maroon, and brown. New leaves begin emerging on hairy stems as the last flowers bloom. These new leaves are almost silver or frosted in appearance.

Two species of Hepatica are found in the United States, those with rounded lobes to their leaves and those with pointed lobes. Occasionally, the leaves may have up to seven additional lobes.

The Hepatica blooms about the same time as the Crocus, and can be quite an enhancement to a shade spring garden, although it also seems to do well on sunny banks and knolls. However, any plants purchased must come from nursery-grown stock and not be taken from the wild.

No spring woodland wildflower garden would be complete without Hepatica. Other flowers in such a garden would include the Harbinger-of-Spring, or Salt-and-Pepper as it is commonly called, which blooms before Hepatica. Blooming along with Hepatica would be the Trout Lily, Spring-beauty, and Toothwort. Later, Dutchman's-breeches, Wild Ginger, Squirrel Corn, and Jack-in-the-Pulpit would bloom. With the Wild Geranium and Violet the spring wildflower garden would be complete.

Hepatica americana

HEPATICA

WOOD SORREL

The Wood Sorrel is sometimes called the Shamrock plant because it has the three-lobed leaves of the Shamrock. Some type of Sorrel may be found everywhere in the United States. The Common Wood and Yellow Wood Sorrel are found in yards, woods, and waste places. The shamrock-shaped leaves are sour to the taste and are sometimes used in salads for flavor. They can grow to be almost two feet tall.

The flower is yellow or pink, with five petals, and is on a separate stalk from the leaves. The flowers give way to seed heads that are cigar-shaped and usually point upward. The plant blooms throughout the growing season, and is a welcome ground cover wherever it occurs.

The Wood Shamrock, as it is sometimes called, often grows in patches along with ferns and mosses. When this plant is not blooming it can still be impressive because of the green bed of shamrock-like leaves it produces. However, the four-leaf clover shape is rarely found in the Wood Sorrel's leaves as it very rarely varies from three leaflets. The Wood Sorrel is associated with the Irish because it is a shade plant, and has a quality of green that is quite unique.

Some of the Copper Butterflies like the sour taste of the leaves, but not as well as they like the Sheep Sorrel. The pink or yellow flowers attract some moths, but are really not preferred by most nectar feeders.

Oxalis europaea

WOOD SORREL

BERGAMOT

The lilac or pinkish flowers of the Bergamot are typical of the Mint family in that they are orchid-like and tubular, with the lower lip curving down. The flowers are clustered on a dense head at the top of the plant. Beneath the flower head are the bracts which can sometimes be colored.

As in the other Mints, the stem is square and the leaves are opposite. The leaves are grayish, triangular, and toothed. The plant gives off a pleasant scent even when just brushed against.

This perennial can grow to about two feet, and is found throughout the eastern United States in well-drained, rich soils. The Bergamot blooms during the summer months. The seed heads remain erect through the winter. Other names for this plant, or similar species, are Oswego-Tea, Bee-balm, Spotted Monarda, and Horsemint. The Bee-balm is a deep red flower which has been cultivated.

Because of its attractiveness to butterflies and hummingbirds Bergamot is used extensively in home landscapes. It will make a thick bed of plants, and spreads by roots and reseeding.

Indians used the leaves of the Bergamot to make Oswego Tea and other special brews when mixed with other herbs. The poultice of this plant was used to treat bee stings. The name Bergamot came from the settler's memory of the strong scent of the bergamo oranges from the old country.

The Bergamot can be grown by harvesting the seed heads and scattering them while working the soil, or from cuttings which have been placed in water or wet sand to start the roots. Of course, digging mature plants and dividing them will give you a head start.

Monarda fistulosa

BERGAMOT

BOUNCING BET

Belonging to the Pink family, the Bouncing Bet is also called Soapwort. If the leaves are crushed and rubbed between the hands with a little water they make a lather, hence the name Soapwort. The one-inch flowers are generally pink, but can be white to pinkish-white. The flowers have five petals that have indented ends or scalloped ends. The flowers bloom in summer to early fall. The leaves are oval and four to six arise from one axis on the stem.

The Bouncing Bet can reach a height of about two feet tall in good growing conditions. It can be found across the entire United States and is common on sand dunes, and in old fields, road-sides, and meadows.

The flower is quite handsome, and a planting of Soapwort will maintain itself and provide a pretty bed of pink, long-lasting flowers.

The plant has long been used to enhance laundry soaps and cleaning concoctions. It has also been used as a herb for certain ailments, even though the sub-stances that make it good for laundry are suspect for the human intestinal tract. Also called the Washer Woman, Bouncing Bet was grown on garden borders for the laundress.

To most of us, the weed is a plant that is out of place or unwanted. But in the natural scheme of things, the weed is a plant that has adapted to soil changes, usually as the result of man's disturbance. The Soap-wort, or Bouncing Bet, falls into this category as a native plant of the ever-shifting sand dunes. The Bouncing Bet grows quickly and produces flowers and seeds as soon as it can.

Saponaria officinalis

110

BOUNCING BET

SWAMP MILKWEED

The flowers of the Swamp Milkweed are similar to those of the Common Milkweed, except for their beautiful pink to rose-pink color. They have the same corolla that sports the down-curved appendages which appear to be petals. The flowers appear in umbels at the top of the plant, and may be several inches across. The opposite leaves are lance-shaped, and much thinner than the Common Milkweed.

The Swamp Milkweed, as its name implies, grows in the moist conditions of marshes and shore-lines. It grows four to six feet in height. It blooms in the summer across the eastern United States. As in the Common Milkweed, the young seed pods and shoots are edible when boiled in numerous changes of water.

This Milkweed also has a milky sap that is extremely bad-tasting, which causes most animals to avoid it. Many insects like the flowers of the Milk-weeds, and a few beetles will actually eat the plant. The Mon-arch caterpillar prefers the Milk-weeds for their host plant, trans-ferring the bitter plant character-istics to themselves. The Mon-arch butterfly also enjoys this unpalatable state and is avoided by all who have tasted its ances-tors. Besides the Monarch and Queen butterflies, which prefer the Milkweed plants for their food plant, some of the Hair-streaks and Blues do as well. However, it is not known how much they use the plant for their food.

The Swamp Milkweed is not normally used in home land-scapes. However, it is used in waterscapes where it is quite pretty. The Swamp Milkweed is one of the exquisite plants of the marsh during the late summer bloom when the marsh becomes a veritable blanket of color. The Swamp Milkweed is the first to bloom, followed by the Joe-Pye-Weed and Boneset. In the early fall, the Ironweed and Sunflower accompany this fantastic array of color. The Swamp Milkweed is the daintiest of this group with its blush of pink and cluster of flowers.

Asclepias incarnata

SWAMP MILKWEED

COMMON MILKWEED

Common Milkweed is one of our native weeds. It is found in pastures, meadows, fields, and roadsides in the eastern United States. The Common Milkweed is not grown horticulturally, but its relative the Butterfly-weed is.

The flower is easy to identify because of its odd shape. The flowers are in clusters arising from the leaf axils at the top of the plant. The flowers have a corolla that is five-parted, with the lobes recurved backward, making them appear to be downward-curving petals. The flowers are usually pink, but can range from nearly white to almost red or even violet.

The flowers give way to seed pods two to four inches long. When the seed pods are ripe they break open along one side and the oval, flat seeds inside fall out and are distributed by the wind on silken parachutes. The leaves are smooth, large, and oblong reaching nearly six to eight inches in length.

The Milkweeds have a bitter, milky sap, hence the name. Young plants and seed pods are edible if boiled in a number of hot water baths to rid the plant of the bitter taste. At least three baths with a total cooking time of more than fifteen minutes are required.

The Monarch butterfly likes the Milkweed because it is a good food and nectar source, but many other insects also favor it, including the Milkweed Bug and the Milkweed Beetle. The Milkweed Beetle is sometimes called the Telephone Bug because if you catch a couple of them, cup them into your hand, shake them up, and then cup the hand over your ear you will hear a sound like the dial tone of a telephone.

Asclepias syriaca

COMMON MILKWEED

BURDOCK

Although it looks somewhat like a thistle head, the Burdock is not a thistle. The one-inch flower head is made up of small, pinkish flowers of lavender or rose-purple. Beneath the flowers are bracts with very bristly hooks which allow the mature seeds to be dispersed as they attach to anything that comes in contact with them.

Anyone who is out-of-doors during the fall will come into contact with the seed heads of the Burdock and the Showy Tick-trefoil. They not only attach to people and animals, but to each other as well, making a big mess especially on socks and mittens.

Children call the Burdock the "Bird's Nest" plant because numerous burs can be hooked together to form the shape of a nest. The Burdock can be a hazard to birds. Records show that Goldfinches and Humming-birds have died in its grasp.

This European weed grows to about five or six feet tall, and can be found in dryer soils that have had some cultivation. It is a biennial, taking two years to produce a flower and seeds. The leaves are large at the base and become progressively smaller towards the top. The flowers bloom from mid-summer through the fall.

The Burdock exhibits a characteristic of many plants that are large-leaved, live in the open, and are vulnerable to grazing. It has a leaf and stem that when torn or broken, not only tastes bad but produces a bad smell as well to discourage potential grazers. The large leaves also shade out any nearby plants. Therefore, the Burdock will be the most successful in getting the sun and moisture from the soil.

The Painted Lady butterfly prefers the Burdock for its food plant, with its larvae feeding upon the leaves.

Arctium minus

BURDOCK

SHOWY TICK-TREFOIL

Every hunter or outdoors man who ventures into the woods and fields during the fall is aware of this plant. The seeds of the Showy Tick-trefoil make themselves known. These seeds, also called 'sticktights,' are about one-quarter inch in length, brown and triangular-shaped. The flat triangles have tiny hooks that attach to anything they touch. This is how the seeds disperse from one area to another.

The plants are in the Pea family, and so have the characteristic pea-shaped flowers arranged on stalks at the top of the plant. The small flowers are light purple or pink in color. The leaves are divided into three leaflets and are smooth-edged. The leaflets are ovate.

The flowers of the Showy Tick-trefoil are, however, not very showy and so are not sought after by the home gardener. The Beggar-tick, as it is also called, adds nitrogen to the soil, as do most of the Pea family and so is a good plant in old fields. It blooms from mid-summer to fall when the nuisance seeds are dispersed to begin new colonies.

The pea-like flower is preferred during the summer by many butterflies such as the Sulphur, Monarch, Fritillaries, Blues, and Coppers. Some Blues and Sulphur butterflies make this plant a host plant. Bees and wasps like the flowers as well, and feed their young with the nectar.

For the Indians, the sticky seeds were a sign that the rut of deer and elk would soon begin and fall would be upon them. They called this the 'season of the riders or carry-ons' because of the propensity of the seeds to stick to everything with which they came into contact.

Desmodium canadense

SHOWY TICK-TREFOIL

SPRING-BEAUTY

The one-half inch pink or white flowers are veined with pink which make them easily identifiable. The six to eight inch plants have two fleshy, grass-like leaves that give rise to the raceme that carries the flowers. As one flower blooms another is growing from a bud to replace it.

A single plant may have numerous flowers during its brief vernal fling before the trees shade the ground. The Spring-beauty only blooms in the spring when it can capture the sun's rays and stores energy in its underground tubers. It can be found in any rich forest situation, but has escaped to some lawns and ditches.

The tubers of this plant give rise to another name, Fairy Spud, because the tubers can be eaten much the same way we eat potatoes. However, it takes many tubers of the Spring-beauty to equal that of a potato, so it does not really challenge the Irish delicacy.

The Spring-beauty makes a good background spring flower because it dies off as summer progresses. Early in the growing season, it is a marvelous flower to have in a shaded lawn. Just make sure you do not mow too early so as to stop the plant from taking up needed energy. The rest of the year you will not know the plants are there.

The Spring-beauty, like many of the spring wildflowers, are truly amazing because they fulfill all the necessary functions for survival in a very short time. They produce flowers, store energy in their bulbs beneath the ground for the next season, and produce a viable seed in just a few short months.

To really appreciate spring wildflowers like the Spring-beauty, it is necessary to follow them from the early spring until their seeds are dispersed and the flowers are dead. Although many people will tell you that spring wildflowers can be found in the late summer they actually are not there, having died back to await another spring.

Claytonia virginica

120

SPRING-BEAUTY

WILD GERANIUM

Also know as the Cranesbill, the Wild Geranium is a common spring wildflower of our forests and open areas. Sometimes the flowers are so abundant that they give a visual sensation of a bed of pink. Although normally pink, the flowers can be colored from lavender to blue or even white. The one-inch five-petaled flower gives way to a seed pod that resembles the bill of a crane, hence the name Cranesbill. The leaves are deeply cleft with three to five lobes with teeth.

An eastern forest plant, the Wild Geranium can be found in most places where there is, or once was, a forest. The potted geranium available at the garden center is a relative, but not a close one. Even though this perennial may transplant well into the shade garden, it never has become extremely popular.

Interestingly, the Wild Geranium was one of the first plants studied to prove that pollen was needed to fertilize plants. Also, the seeds are unusual. As they dry, extreme tension is placed on the pod, which explodes and scatters the seeds yards away.

The Wild Geranium belongs to a large group of flowers which look similar. Many times the novice root hunter will confuse the root of the Wild Ginseng or Wild Ginger with that of the Wild Geranium. They are all quite thick and have many branches. It is best to study the leaves to differentiate these different plants from each other.

Indians used the root as a medicine, grinding it and making a powder to be taken with other teas and potions.

Geranium maculatum

WILD GERANIUM

FIREWEED

This plant grows from Missouri to northern Pennsylvania, as well as in the mountains of Virginia. It is common in burned-over fields and forests, hence the name Fireweed. It can also be found in clearings and disturbed areas. The sight of a field of magenta Fireweed in full bloom after a fire is extremely striking.

A member of the Primrose family, Fireweed exhibits many of the same characteristics, with the four-petaled flowers blooming up racemes at the top of the plant. The flowers are magenta to rose-pink. The flowers bloom upwards followed by cigar-shaped seed pods, both found on the same stem along with new buds forming at the terminus. Old timers say that when the flowers reach the top a frost will occur.

The leaves are long, slender, and lance-shaped. The seed pods give off seeds that have a downy parachute on them. The fall plants are quite striking when the pods open, making them appear frosted.

Other names for Fireweed are Willow Herb and Blooming Sally. The leaves have been used to make a tea to cure colds and whooping cough. The leaves were also used as a poultice for bruises and sore muscles. The young plant has been used as a substitute for Asparagus.

The Red Admiral, a common and beautiful butterfly, likes the nectar of the Fireweed, seemingly above all other flowers. This butterfly is quite tame and will allow you to approach closely. The base color of the Red Admiral is black, with an orange-red band passing through the forewing and trailing into the lower edge of the hindwing. The forewing has white and blue spots in the outer portions. The food plant of the Red Admiral is the Stinging Nettle.

Although the Fireweed is quite attractive, little attention has been given it for the home landscape.

Epilobium angustifolium

124

FIREWEED

DAME'S ROCKET

This escapee from garden plantings has adapted itself well over the eastern United States. It is also called the Cemetery Plant because it is so popular in cemetery plantings around grave stones. Some have also called the Dame's Rocket the Poor Man's Phlox because from a distance it appears phlox-like. The flower color is quite variable, ranging from whites and pinks to violets and blues. This biennial may have flowers of different colors in the same colony.

Since it is part of the Mustard family, the one-inch flowers have the four petals of the cross. They are borne in a cluster at the top of the plant. Seed pods are long and cigar-shaped. The leaves are lance-shaped, toothed, and alternate. The plants spread by seeds so a colony may exist after a couple of seasons. These spring and early summer plants are quite impressive when seen as a colony of two-foot flowers of multiple colors.

Being a Mustard, the seeds are high in protein and oils which are beneficial to wildlife such as birds and mice. The Dame's Rocket is quite aromatic and so attracts bees and butterflies.

Because of its resemblance to phlox, and the great amount of nectar in the flower it is visited by many butterflies.

The Dame's Rocket can be found in a great variety of habitats which encourage different butterflies to frequent this plant. In the open, it will attract the Fritillaries and Sulphurs, while in wooded areas it will attract the Swallowtails as well as some Hairstreaks. The Sulphurs will occasionally use this plant for a food source.

Because of the availability of numerous colors and types of phlox, the Dame's Rocket has lost much of its attraction for the home garden.

Hesperis matronalis

DAME'S ROCKET

EVERLASTING PEA

This escapee from gardens is found only in the northern part of the United States, and south to a line about even with southern Virginia. The Everlasting Pea is a perennial that was used in home landscaping, but now has escaped to the wild. It can be found growing along roadsides, fallow fields, and in waste places with rich soils. This large vine may grow up on poles or trees, but normally is strong enough with its own branches to reach four or five feet.

The oval leaves or leaflets are paired from a stem that has broad wings. These wings make the stems appear to be much more substantial than they really are. The stems produce tendrils like all peas, but they really do not aid this plant.

The pea-shaped flowers are purple or pink in color, sometimes with white in them. Occasionally the flowers may be all white. The flowers are quite large, making this a striking plant even from a distance.

The Everlasting Pea adds nitrogen to the soil and the stems make a good mulch. This would be a good plant to use to cover an unused corner of your yard.

Obtaining seeds from wild pea plants is the best way to introduce this plant.

Both the peas and beans have been used for years as a vine of beautiful flowers grown on trellises on the edges of vegetable gardens. They have been hybridized to provide beautiful colors in the flowers as well as attractive leaves for the garden.

The Everlasting Pea and its relatives attract butterflies and hummingbirds. The Sphinx Moth, or Hawk Moth, is attracted to this plant, but unfortunately one of the Hawk Moths produces the Tomato Hornworm which can wreak havoc with a tomato garden. The Hawk Moth has also been called the Hummingbird Moth because of the way it hovers and gets nectar from the Pea flowers. The Gray Hairstreak and a couple of Blues make the Pea a food plant.

Lathyrus latifolius

128

EVERLASTING PEA

KNOTWEEDS

Another name for this common group of plants is Smartweed. This group has numerous plants found over the entire United States, blooming from early summer through the fall. These plants have several characteristics which make them easy to identify. The name Knotweed comes from the "knot" found at each leaf joint. When coupled with the tight clusters of tiny, pink flowers at the end of the plant or at the leaf axils it is easily identifiable. The leaves are smooth and can be oval or lance-shaped.

These plants are extremely variable when it comes to growing conditions, although most require a fair amount of sun. Some are aquatic, with the flower heads coming above water or the entire plant coming out of the water. One variety has leaves with small, sharp hooks which will tear skin, hence the name Tear Thumb. Other Knotweeds are just common garden weeds.

A member of the Buckwheat family, these plants can be viny or appear to be so. They produce copious amounts of rich seeds which are highly valued by wildlife. The aquatic varieties provide seeds for ducks and other waterfowl. The Smartweeds are not cultivated.

Knotweeds are good food for a number of butterflies including the Coppers, Blues, and Common Sootywing. Since the Knotweed is found in nearly every type of habitat, we can expect to see some of these butterflies nearby. None of the butterflies are very large, but they are quite striking in color and in their habits. The Blues, of course, are blue on the upper parts of the wing while the under colors of the wing are just as striking, although not nearly as bright. The quick Coppers are much the same. Even though they dash about quickly they can be approached if you are quiet and careful.

Polygonum (species)

KNOTWEED

KNAPWEED

Although this plant appears to be similar to the Pasture Thistle, it does not have any spines. The bright, pink flowers are supported on a knob of bracts that appears to have spines. They look spine-like because the bracts are outlined in black. This plant of the Daisy family has a head of flowers which are tubular. The ray flowers are sterile. The leaves are alternate and deeply pinnately dissected, with the lobes being very long and lance-shaped. The leaves give the Knapweed an almost lacy or fern-like appearance.

This import from Europe is found across the United States in fields and on roadsides. It has become especially well-adapted to drier areas of meadows and openings. A few different types of Knapweed are found throughout the eastern United States, having the same basic flower head ranging in color from purple to pink and sometimes white.

Knapweed blooms from mid-summer through September when it produces seeds. The seeds are eaten by birds, but are not necessarily preferred by them. Being a couple of feet tall, the Knapweed does provide food during the winter.

The Bachelor Button is the only ornamental plant from this group used in home landscaping.

Because of the long season of Knapweed it is quite popular as a nectar source. Among the butterflies that prefer this plant are the Skippers, Sulphurs, Checkered White, and Painted Lady. The Painted Lady also uses the Knapweed as a food plant. The most striking thing about the Painted Lady is the color of the underparts of the wings which are a soft mixture of pinks, blacks, and tans scattered with black dots and eyes. The Painted Lady was once called the Thistle Butterfly because of its preference for thistle-like flowers, of which the Knapweed is one.

Centaurea maculosa

132

KNAPWEED

BULL THISTLE

This weed pest is an import from Europe where it is considered a royal plant by the Scots. Actually, when the weedy nature of the plant is taken away, it is quite beautiful and beneficial.

The large flowers which may reach up to three inches across are pretty pink to rose-purple in color. The compound flower is held within a head of spiny bracts that protect it from unsuspecting foragers. The leaves are lance-shaped with teeth ending in sharp spines. The stem is also very spiny. This plant may grow over four feet tall.

Preferring old fields, pastures, and meadows, the Bull Thistle is common over all the United States. The flower is rich in nectar and attracts many butter-flies, bees, and hummingbirds. The flower blooms from June through September. Once a flower has bloomed, it produces numerous seeds that disperse on little parachutes called "thistle-down." It is believed the Ameri-can Goldfinch waits till the seeds of the thistles are produced so it can line its nest with this mate-rial. The seeds are also preferred by the Goldfinch. This biennial seeds itself readily.

As with the Knapweed, the Bull Thistle is used as a food source by the larvae of the Painted Lady. The nectar is preferred by the Painted Lady butterfly as well. The Painted Lady migrates north from the southern states where it overwin-ters as an adult.

Although not necessarily sought after for the perennial bed, the Bull Thistle is an added attraction if left to grow to matu-rity where it may volunteer.

Cirsium vulgare

BULL THISTLE

PASTURE THISTLE

Although similar to the Bull Thistle, the Pasture Thistle is readily distinguishable from it because it does not have the large spines on the stem. Another difference is that the flowers of the Pasture Thistle are larger, many times exceeding three inches across. The Pasture Thistle prefers soil that is dry, and can be found in meadows and pastures in the northern two-thirds of the eastern United States.

The Goldfinches also love the seed of this thistle and use the thistledown for nest building. Since this thistle blooms from June through September, the Goldfinches nest relatively late in the summer nesting season, beginning in the last part of July and ending in mid-August. Because Goldfinches are primarily seed eaters, the thistle plants are a good food source for baby Goldfinches.

Commercial establishments offer 'thistle,' or finch food, to feed the Goldfinches during the winter. You need not fear that you will end up with a yard full of thistle plants as this seed, also called "niger," is actually an imported small sunflower. It has a difficult time growing in our climate.

Probably no plants have as much success as the thistles in attracting butterflies. Butterflies use their long proboscises to probe for the nectar in the beautiful flowers. The Dogface Butterfly, Tortoise Shell, Painted Lady, Red Admiral, Monarch, Skippers, all of the Fritillaries, and of course, the mimic Viceroy all prefer the nectar of the thistle. Photographers have known for years that to take good pictures of butterflies you must get them to sit still. The butterflies seem to be mesmerized while taking nectar from the thistle. To take good pictures just set up your tripod, focus on the best thistle flowers, and wait. In just a short time, you will be rewarded with a long visit from a butterfly.

Cirsium pumilum

136

PASTURE THISTLE

CANADA THISTLE

The Canada Thistle is the most hated of all thistles because it is very invasive and hard to eradicate. Growing over the entire United States, this thistle has the typical flower head with numerous pink or purple flowers held up by a bulb covered with spiny bracts. However, the flower heads of the Canada Thistle are smaller than the Bull or Pasture Thistle, being only about one inch in diameter.

Nevertheless, the flowers are rich in nectar and are visited by a wide variety of bees and butterflies. The leaves of this thistle are long, lance-shaped, and extremely spiny. The stem of the Canada Thistle is smooth. Like the other thistles, the Canada Thistle blooms through the summer.

Thistles evolved spines to protect them from animals who would make a meal of them. To offset the discouraging effect of the defensive spines, the thistles therefore produce beautiful flowers with flower heads rich in nectar to attract butterflies and bees for purposes of pollination. The seeds are also adapted to be dispersed by wind, without help from animals or birds. For instance, Goldfinches disperse the seeds when they use the thistle-down for their nests. It appears that the only animal that will eat the thistle plant is the larvae of the Painted Lady butterfly.

Being a very weedy thistle, the Canada Thistle should not be allowed to grow in the yard. The Bull or Pasture Thistle would be a better choice should one wish to encourage a thistle plant. Eradication should be done with repeated tilling or a safe herbicide. Mulching the seed heads in the compost pile may not destroy their viability.

Cirsium arvense

CANADA THISTLE

JOE-PYE-WEED

Similar to the Ironweed, the Joe-Pye-Weed has an umbel of flowers forming a head. The pink flowers are also small, but usually greater in number than the Ironweed. The leaves of the two plants are similar, but the leaves of the Joe-Pye-Weed are whorled with three to seven leaves arising from the same region on the stem. The six-foot stem also has red or purple coloring at the joints. The Joe-Pye-Weed begins blooming in late July and continues until September. These plants can be commonly found in wet areas over the entire eastern United States.

Joe-Pye was an Indian who wished to be a medicine man. One day he was called to heal a young boy with a bone injury. The herb he needed was called Boneset, but when Joe-Pye went into the marsh to obtain the Boneset he mistook the Joe-Pye-Weed for it. The Joe-Pye-Weed did not work and the boy did not get well. The Indian gods became very angry and they turned Joe-Pye into the plant he had collected. That is where he is today, the Joe-Pye-Weed.

Actually there were a number of medicinal uses credited to the Joe-Pye-Weed. Most of these where made from the leaves which were used in teas which were said to cure everything from arthritis to fevers.

The Joe-Pye-Weed has not normally been utilized in home landscapes except possibly in the natural water garden.

Among the butterflies that prefer the Joe-Pye-Weed for nectar are the Admirals and Viceroy. The Viceroy is unique because it mimics the Monarch butterfly. It does this because the Monarch uses the Milkweed family for their food plants, from which they pick up a bad taste. This bad taste gives them an advantage over other butterflies because birds learn not to eat the Monarch.

The two butterflies can be distinguished by size and coloring. The Viceroy is smaller, and has a black line that runs across the top of the hind wing that the Monarch does not have. Since the Viceroy does not eat the Milkweed it does not have the taste that birds dislike, but because it resembles a Monarch, birds leave it alone.

Eupatorium purpureum

140

JOE-PYE-WEED

CUT-LEAVED TOOTHWORT

The Cut-leaved Toothwort has a cluster of four-petaled, white flowers at the terminal end of the plant. The flowers may be pink, especially after being in bloom for a few days. Three deeply-cut, toothed leaves arise from the stem below the flowers. The leaves may have from three to five leaflets, with the plant growing about one foot tall.

The Toothwort may be found in rich forests, streamsides, and bottomlands over the entire eastern United States. Being a spring wildflower it must get its flowers and leaves up before the sunlight is blocked by the leaves of the trees, whereupon the plant dies back.

As in so many of the Mustard plants, the roots of this plant gives off a peppery or horse-radishy flavor, giving rise to the names Pepperwort and Wild Horseradish. The tooth-shaped roots are that to which the genus *Dentaria* refers. According to the Doctrine of Signatures, this plant can cure toothaches.

The Cut-leaved Toothwort is a great spring wildflower to have in your understory. It grows readily once transplanted, and becomes quite prolific. The flowers add a welcome blanket of color to the spring landscape.

The Purple Spring Cress is related to the Cut-leaved Tooth-wort, but blooms later in the spring and has purplish flowers and more of a basal rosette of leaves.

This early spring wildflower is visited by the Mourning Cloak and the Spring Azure butterflies. The Spring Azure uses this plant for food as well as nectar. The West Virginia White, Checkered White, and the Common Sulphur have also been known to use the Toothwort as a food plant, as well as others of the Mustard family.

Dentaria laciniata

CUT-LEAVED TOOTHWORT

BINDWEED

Similar to the Morning Glory, the Bindweed has a funnel-shaped flower. The flowers can be pink or white. The Field Bindweed may have pink stripes in the white flower.

The major difference between the two plants is in the leaves. The leaves of the Bindweed are arrow-shaped instead of heart-shaped like the leaves of the Morning Glory.

The Bindweed is common in hedgerows, waysides, ditches, and old fields. This vine may grow to be fifteen to twenty feet long, and is very aggressive on the ground. It entwines everything that it comes in contact with, sometimes killing the other plants. No doubt this is where the name Bindweed comes from, indicating being bound against one's will.

Atlhough the Bindweed can be used to attract butterflies and hummingbirds, the Morning Glory is better suited for the garden. The Bindweed is very aggressive, and will soon take over the corner of the garden it is planted in, to the detriment of the other plants. Killing or controlling this plant is also very difficult. Tilling the plant without getting all the pieces will only permit those pieces to produce new plants.

The plant has been used as tea before breakfast to provide a gentle laxative. Indians used the plant as a poultice to cure wounds and draw out boils.

Many butterflies and moths use the flowers of the Bindweed for nectar. The long, tubular flowers are especially well-adapted to their long proboscises. Although not as aromatic as the Morning Glories, the Bindweed can also be used for nectar by hummingbirds, especially in times of low flower blooms.

Convolvulus sepium

BINDWEED

PEPPERMINT

The Peppermint, as well as the Spearmint, belong in the Mint family. They exhibit the characteristics of the Mint family in their square stems, opposite leaves, and orchid-like flowers. The Peppermint has flowers that arise on bracts from the leaf axils. The flowers are pink, and are arranged in whorls on the bracts.

Peppermint can grow to three feet high, and prefers the moist areas around lakes, streams, ditches, and wet meadows. It has a purple stem and grows rather vigorously by underground shoots. Peppermint was cultivated extensively in this country, being grown in massive fields, usually a reclaimed wetland, that could be kept moist. It was then harvested and crushed for the oil extract.

All the Mints are herbal and have some aromatic oils associated with them. However, some are not necessarily pleasant to encounter. The odor of the Mint can be smelled for miles. Many times the mulch was mixed with hay for cattle, which in turn, gave even their manure a minty smell. Synthetic flavorings eventually made Mints less economical to grow.

Peppermint is easy to grow from cuttings and makes a good border with its pretty flowers. If the plants get bruised a smell of mint is given off. The leaves are often picked and added to a Mint Julep or a refreshing glass of iced tea. Many mints are used as ornamentals in our gardens.

The Gray Hairstreak butterfly uses the Peppermint for its food plant. The Hairstreak is gray all over with a streak of hair trailing from the hindwing. It has large spots of orange and blue where the hair originates. The underwing color is a soft, silver-gray, with two parallel lines of black that follow the outer wing, and orange spots showing through. The Gray Hairstreak also uses the cotton plant for its food plant and is sometimes called the Cotton Borer.

Mentha piperita

PEPPERMINT

LOOSESTRIFE

Flowers from these two species can be found throughout the eastern United States, usually in moist, rich soils. The flower of the Purple Loosestrife is purple-pink in color. This immigrant from Europe has moved into the wetlands of the United States with a vengeance, crowding out beneficial species. Although this plant makes a beautiful ornamental plant for well-tended perennial gardens, because of the invasive nature of this plant some states have banned its sale.

The Purple Loosestrife grows about three feet tall, and all its flowers are on the top of the stem. A field of these flowers is quite impressive and would be beautiful except for the fact that it is harming our native species.

The Yellow Loosestrife is mostly native and also prefers moist soils. The leaves are usually whorled with the five-petaled flowers arising from the leaf axils. There is also a Yellow Loosestrife, called Garden Loosestrife, that has escaped from cultivation. These two Yellow Loosestrifes are different from the Purple Loosestrife, as they do not become invasive.

The Loosestrifes are said to act as a sedative for animals and people. Chewing the leaves it is said, will make you 'loose your strife.' Even though this plant has been used over the years as a potion, no real evidence exists as to its validity as a medicinal aid.

Many of the Loosestrifes are ornamentally grown, but the wild varieties are sometimes quite invasive and are not recommended for the home gardener. Propagation of the Wild Loosestrife is best done by transplanting one plant at a time, and harvesting the flowers before they mature. This keeps the seed source from spreading. Some of the unique varieties that could be used in the backyard garden are the Swamp Candle, Whorled Loosestrife, and Tufted Loosestrife. The Tufted Loosestrife can be grown in some shade.

Lysimachia and Lythrum (species)

148

LOOSESTRIFE

WILD COLUMBINE

A favorite of the hummingbird, this nodding woodland flower prefers rich soil but will do well in moderately rich, sandy soil. The Columbine can be found throughout the entire eastern United States.

The flowers of this perennial are yellow and scarlet-red with long petals that extend upward to make long spurs with a bulb at the end. The leaves are three-lobed with scalloped edges. The long flower of the Columbine can only be pollinated by moths and hummingbirds because of these long tubes. Since it is attractive to hummingbirds it is a favorite in the perennial garden, giving it a late spring beauty.

Even though this plant is a perennial it usually needs to be replaced after a few years, even though it does readily reseed itself. Seeds can be collected in the fall from the slender pods that split open as the seeds mature. Shaking the pods will cause numerous shiny, black seeds to spill out. These can be scattered in the flower bed in the fall and in a couple of years there will be a continuous supply of seeds and plants. Several varieties of Columbine have been hybridized for the garden, but seem to have more trouble reseeding themselves, and must be replanted periodically.

As summer progresses and the seed of the Columbine begins to ripen, a tiny insect called the Leaf Miner sometimes makes its way into the leaf and eats its way along the inner layers. The leaf becomes translucent wherever the Leaf Miner has eaten. The life of this insect can be followed as it grows, making a larger tunnel as it eats it way around the leaf. Eventually it will become large enough so that it will drop out of the leaf. A number of plants in this group have this type of pest. However, since the season is nearly over the plant is probably not affected.

Indians used the Columbine for several medicinal cures, as a love potion, and even prepared it as a cologne for men.

Aquilegia canadensis

150

WILD COLUMBINE

RED CLOVER

Although it looks very similar to the White Clover, the Red Clover is larger and has a stalkless, rose-red flower. This plant can be found in meadows and fields that have been fallow for a long time. The flower heads may reach one inch across, and the plant may grow to more than two feet tall. The three leaflets usually have a light green 'vee' pattern in them, making them quite attractive as well. The plant blooms continuously through the summer. If you take the time to dissect a flower head, you will find the individual flowers are like pea-like and quite pretty.

The Red Clover can be found throughout the United States in the mesic soils of meadows, and are old friends on the edges of our gardens where the soil has not been disturbed for awhile.

The Red Clover was probably brought from Europe as a hay crop. Since the Red Clover grows larger than our native White Clover, it is much sought after for its nitrogen and protein content. The Red Clover is a good forage plant for cattle, and the blossoms are extremely attractive to honeybees. As in all the Clovers, these plants add nitrogen to the soil, and therefore are an asset as a cover crop or a crop that is tilled into the soil to add mulch and nitrogen. The best use for Red Clover is probably the enhancement of garden soil, although the added benefit of attracting numerous butterflies to the nectar-rich flowers is well worth the planting by itself.

Being an open-sun perennial, the Red Clover is the favorite nectar flower of many butterflies. Some of the butterflies that use it for a food plant are the Sulphurs, Blues, and some Skippers. Although many Skippers use the flowers for nectar they are usually associated with the Red Clover because of the accompanying grasses which are a favorite of the Skipper's larval stages.

Seeds may be obtained from your local garden center or farm store. The Red Clover will flourish in a variety of soils and is easily grown from seed.

Trifolium pratense

RED CLOVER

SHEEP SORREL

Most farm children know this weed from Europe as Sour Weed or Sour Grass. It came by this name because of the sour taste of the new green leaves. It is said to refresh one's thirst if chewed. It can be found growing in waste areas, old fields, roadsides, and dry meadows.

The Sheep Sorrel does not get very tall, usually less than a foot, but it does make a handsome colony of plants when it gets a chance. The short stalks of red flowers in a group give the landscape a red glow, so much so that the unknowing must walk over to see what is causing this red color. The flowers are very tiny, but the abundance of them makes up for their lack of size.

The leaves of the Sheep Sorrel are arrow-shaped with two pointed leaves at the base. The leaves make a basal rosette from which the plant raises the raceme of flowers. Blooms continue from June through fall. It is not a plant we want in our gardens and getting rid of it can be difficult.

The three specific butterflies that make the Sheep Sorrel their food plant are the American Copper, the Lustrous Copper of the West, and the Small Copper.

The American Copper is found throughout the eastern United States, except in the extreme southern states of Florida, Alabama, and Mississippi. Not only is this small butterfly a lovely copper color, it is quite beautiful on the underside of its wings, being pale sky-blue with orange and black spots.

With a little luck you might be able to collect some of the green larvae and rear some of these beautiful butterflies. More likely, however, it would be easier to collect the chrysalis in the fall from a large patch of Sheep Sorrel. Other Coppers and Blues will make use of this plant for their nectar.

Rumex acetosella

154

SHEEP SORREL

WHITE CLOVER

This clover is probably the most common clover found in our yards. In fact, it grows in virtually every grassy expanse. It is a welcome addition to the lawn as it is a legume, a plant that adds nitrogen to the soil. This low-growing flower, usually less than one foot tall, can be found throughout the United States. The flowers can be almost pink when blooming.

Most often it is the White Clover that produces the rarity of a four-leaf clover. Occasionally, you may find several four-leaf clover leaves on the same plant or even five or six-leaf clover leaves. If you locate such a plant the likelihood is that it will continue to produce these odd leaves for years to come.

The flower heads have been used over the years as a garnish in salads, and as a spice to flavor tobacco, cheeses, and tea. Its abundance makes it especially attractive to rabbits, chipmunks, butterflies, and bees. Deer and cattle prefer the clovers for food along with the grasses and alfalfa.

White Clover is often added to grass seed to give some body to lawns, as well as to add nitrogen to the soil. Although a welcome addition to the yard, the White Clover is not particularly a landscape flower and is better used as a background plant in grassy areas.

The short flowers of the White Clover allow the honeybee to take nectar from the seed blossoms. This clover is sought by many beekeepers to produce what many say is the best-flavored honey.

Of course, we can't forget the shamrock myth of St. Patrick who supposedly chose the shamrock with its three leaves to represent the Trinity.

Trifolium repens

WHITE CLOVER

MAY-APPLE

The May-apple is found over the entire eastern United States where rich forest soils exist. Occasionally they are found in open areas or fencerows. Sometimes called Umbrella Leaf by children, the May-apple looks like it has two umbrellas hanging over the white flower. Having six to nine petals, the two-inch flower hangs down from the axis of the two leaves. The leaves are deeply cut with five to seven lobes. The plant grows underground, shooting up a stem producing either one or two leaves on a stalk. Only the stalks with two leaves produce a flower and fruit. The colony of plants may exceed a half acre.

The fruit is poisonous, as is the rest of the plant, until it ripens to a brownish-yellow. Some make jelly from the fruit when ripe. The fruit gets to be about the size of a walnut as summer progresses, and the leaves die down. Even though the plant is poisonous, many potions were made from it and it was mostly used as a cathartic.

Although not easily grown, this plant does make a good landscape plant when found in the yard. It can sometimes be started by root stock.

The May-apple has the same characteristics that most spring ephemerals do. They bloom early before the sun is hidden by the leaves of the forest, mature during the early summer, and die back as summer progresses. The May-apple has large leaves which allow it to capture the sun more efficiently, and therefore to remain alive longer than many of the other spring wildflowers. It will produce a large fruit from the beautiful white flower.

The May-apple, with its umbrella-like leaves, is a favorite of wildlife artists who seem to think that the leaves should be covering a toad, chipmunk, or even a mythical elf on note cards and small prints.

Podophyllum peltatum

158

MAY-APPLE

BLADDER CAMPION/CATCHFLY

Plants in this group have a large oblong bulb behind the five-flower petals. The petals are white, deeply notched, and are usually perpendicular to the bulb end. The color of the flower can be white approaching pink. The flowers are about one-half inch long, while the plant may reach nearly two feet in height. The opposite leaves are oval and almost clasp the stem.

The Catchfly, or Bladder Campion, can be found throughout the eastern United States in most fields and disturbed areas. This is a weed we have inherited from Europe.

It is named Catchfly because the bulb behind the flower sometimes catches insects and appears to devour them. However, this is not the case with the Catchfly, as they merely become entrapped. On the other hand, the Pitcher Plant does digest the insects it traps.

The Evening Lychnis is similar to the Bladder Campion, and is a late spring and summer plant. Another cultivated variety is the Nightflowering Catchfly. This pretty plant was used in old gardens, but has escaped to the wild along with the Rose Campion. If you can find these, they make wonderful additions to the perennial bed.

The long bladder behind the flower petals makes this flower almost exclusively the favorite of butterflies and moths. They are the only ones with long enough proboscises to reach into the flower to obtain the nectar. There are a few robber insects which bypass the flower head and bore a hole in the side of the Campion to reach the nectar, but they are few and probably do not aid in fertilization.

The seeds are not edible to humans, but some wildlife eats them. A couple of beetles will eat the mature seeds by chewing through the capsule before the seeds are dried.

Silene cucubalus

160

BLADDER CAMPION/CATCHFLY

BLOODROOT

The Bloodroot is one of the earliest spring wildflowers. It is found in the rich soils of wooded areas throughout the eastern United States, except for the very far northeast.

This white flower can be almost two inches across as it emerges from the clasp of leaves that surround it. The Bloodroot takes advantage of the spring sun, when there are no leaves on the trees, to build energy it then stores in its roots. The eight white petals are very fragile, and close in any adversity of temperature or lights. In most areas it is done blooming by the end of May. The leaves are a silky green while emerging, but upon opening they become dark green. The leaves are deeply-lobed with five to nine lobes. The leaves will eventually become about ten inches tall by mid-summer.

Bloodroot gets its name from the bright red sap that it exudes when it is injured. Indians used the sap as a dye for clothing and other artifacts. They also used the dye to paint themselves for different occasions. There were some medicinal uses attributed to the Bloodroot, but as it is poisonous these were minimal.

The Bloodroot is quite showy in the very early spring and later the leaves make a good understory ground cover. This makes the plant attractive to a woodland landscape setting.

It is easy to collect the seeds of the Bloodroot, as the flower petals fall off to reveal the seed capsule. The leaves will continue to grow, sometimes overshadowing the capsule. The seed capsules are ripe when they are quite swollen and exhibit a tinge of yellow or brown. The seeds may not be viable if they are stored. A bit of moist soil should be put in with the capsules until they open and release the seeds. It takes about a month for the capsule to ripen. The seeds must be sown in rich soil.

The plants can also be grown from the rhizomes, but this method tends to be less successful than propagation by seed. Obtaining the plants from a reputable grower may be the best way to initially begin your Bloodroot patch. These plants should not be removed from the wild.

Sanguinaria canadensis

BLOODROOT

LARGE-FLOWERED TRILLIUM

This large, white flower is found in areas that are wooded or recently have been wooded. The Trillium is the largest of its group with three white petals, three leaves, and three sepals. A spring wildflower, it usually is finished blooming as the forest canopy becomes full. As the flowers mature they may take on a pink to red color, which may cause them to be confused with the Red Trilliums. The Large-flowered Trillium can be found in forests throughout the eastern United States.

This plant does best in rich, woodland soils with a constant supply of moisture in the humus. It is the easiest Trillium to grow in our yards and it makes a pretty addition to a woodland landscape. As in so many woodland wildflowers, the root stalk must provide the next year's growth, so picking the flower will kill the plant. These plants should never be taken from the wild.

Indians used the roots of the Trillium for treating many minor illnesses, such as upset stomach, sore joints, toothache, and earaches. The medicinal uses are not verified today, and its use is not recommended because it would of necessity kill the plant.

A spring forest, alive with the Large-flowered Trillium, creates an excitement that always makes a gardener say, "I want those in my woodland garden." Luckily numerous reputable growers produce this flower as well as other trilliums.

The Trillium blooms later in the spring than many of the spring wildflowers, and so requires a bit of monitoring to collect mature seed. About six weeks after the flower blooms the seed will be mature. The seed head is oblong with the characteristic three parts of the Trillium plant. The pulpy, white fruit ripens and splits about late June when the seed is brown in color. This is an opportune time for collection.

The seeds should be sown immediately. If the seeds are to be stored, they should be kept in a refrigerator with a bit of moisture. It may take four to seven years for a plant, started from seed, to produce a flower. When harvesting seeds, care should be taken not to hurt the leaf, as it produces energy for the plant's future growth and viability.

Trillium grandiflorum

LARGE-FLOWERED TRILLIUM

QUEEN ANNE'S LACE

Everyone knows the Queen Anne's Lace, which is also called the Bird's Nest Flower, Wild Carrot or Winter Lace. One reason it is called Wild Carrot is because the leaves, stems, and roots taste and smell like that of the carrot, although tasting a bit bitter.

The name Bird's Nest Flower is due to its flower head, which turns up into a cup, resembling that of a small bird's nest, once the flower has gone to seed. This nest remains erect all winter and is beautiful with a crown of snow on it. The seeds are eaten by many types of wildlife, but are not preferred by them.

Found throughout the entire eastern United States, this three-foot plant has flat, white flower heads that can reach four inches in width. The flower head is actually a large cluster of flowers, sometimes with a deep purple, center floweret. The purple center may help attract insects for pollination. These insects are predatory and are looking for an easy meal, so they will "stalk" the center floweret thinking it is another insect. Research seems to indicate those that have the purple center have a higher degree of pollination success.

Being a biennial, the first year's growth looks like that of a carrot, while the root stores energy from the lacy, fern-like leaves. In the second season, the flower emerges and produces the seeds. This plant is quite determined to produce seeds once it has established a root. Repeated mowings will only produce smaller and smaller flowerheads, until the root is exhausted.

Some medicinal uses existed but were not widespread. Because of the carotin in the plant, it was probably of some actual benefit. Today its use is limited to dried flower arrangements. One particularly pretty use is to dry the flowers while they are in full bloom, and then sprinkle them with small, silver sparkles secured with hair spray. This makes an elegant, long-lasting, lacy flower for an arrangement.

Because of the weedy nature of Queen Anne's Lace, and the fact that it grows nearly everywhere in dry soil, it is not used as a cultivated ornamental plant.

Daucus carota

QUEEN ANNE'S LACE

WHITE BANEBERRY

A flower of the forest, the White Baneberry grows in rich soils. It can be found as far south as the southern Appalachians. Reaching a height of almost two feet, the plants produce a single stalk of tightly-clustered flowers. The individual flowers are small, with about four to ten white petals. The leaves are twice-divided and toothed.

Another name for the White Baneberry is Doll's Eye from the white berries produced on a red stalk. These berries are about one-half inch long and pure white with a black dot at the end. It is said that they resemble the eyes of a china doll.

The Baneberry is a spring wildflower that blooms later in the spring than other spring flowers such as the Spring-beauty, and can last into the summer and even into the fall. Because the White Baneberry is taller than the other spring flowers, it catches more sunlight. Even though the leaves are not large, they are numerous, making them more efficient in capturing the light. Also, the leaves surround the plant so that no light will be missed or pass through to the ground. Leaves at a lower level than others are staggered to permit the light to get to them.

Given the size of the White Baneberry, the berries and seed are not extremely large, which also helps it survive during the times of low light from the overhead canopy. The mature, white berries can be collected in early fall and should be sown directly into the soil for best germinating success. If they are to be stored, they should be placed in moist soil and allowed to go through a winter cold period.

The White Baneberry is generally not used in garden landscapes, as the plant and the berries are poisonous. In fact, the roots were used as a strong purgative. Before planting the Baneberries, you should give serious consideration to the poisonous nature of the berries. The red ones are especially attractive to children.

Actaea pachypoda

WHITE BANEBERRY

FALSE SOLOMON'S-SEAL

The only reason the word "false" is in the name of this plant is that it is not the true Solomon's-seal. They are somewhat difficult to tell apart when not in bloom, because the leaf patterns are similar. The major difference between them is that the False Solomon's-seal has its small, white flowers clustered at the end of the plant on racemes, whereas the Solomon's-seal has the flowers hanging down from each leaf axil.

The plant grows as a long plume and is unbranched with alternating leaves. The leaves are oblong, heavily-veined, and almost parallel. The stem takes a slight bend at each leaf giving the plant a zig-zag pattern, which gives rise to another name, the Solomon's Zig-Zag.

False Solomon's-seal is common over the entire United States in rich woods and forest edges. It sometimes will grow in full sun. Easily transplanted, this flower makes a good understory plant for the shade garden and garden edges. False Solomon's-seal spreads by roots, and so will quickly make a dense bed of long graceful plume-like plants.

Plumed Solomon's-seal is another name for this plant because of this graceful plume of flowers.

The berries turn to a reddish-brown and are relished by birds and other wildlife. People have been known to eat the berries, however not extensively. When crushed the berries give off a pleasant odor.

The False Solomon's-seal is a great plant to put in a woodland garden that has a lot of shade. It can be coupled with a number of ferns and smaller flowers such as the Foam Flower, Stone Crop, and Bluebells. You may wish to mix the False Solomon's-seal with the Solomon's-seal to make a striking contrast.

Smilacina racemosa

170

FALSE SOLOMON'S SEAL

CHICKWEED

Every gardener knows the Chickweed. It spreads through our gardens very quickly if we do not keep up our weeding. Even though it seems easy to pull and destroy it, it is successful in coming back from just a few plant parts left in the soil and from the many seeds it has produced over the years. This plant is common over the entire United States in cultivated soils and waste places that have been disturbed.

Although the Chickweed does not grow very tall, it can get to a length of a couple of feet, usually becoming prostrate. The leaves are oval and opposite. The small flowers are interesting to look at, producing five petals that appear as if there were ten because they are deeply cleft. The anthers are quite tall and sometimes make the petals appear speckled.

As with most weeds, the Chickweeds are very good at producing seeds that are much liked by birds. On old farmsteads, the chickens seemed to like these seeds, which gives credence to the name Chickweed. The leaves can be used as greens in salads, but are better tasting when cooked like spinach. Since this plant blooms from the time it emerges in the spring, it is used extensively by wildlife, both for its leaves as well as its seeds.

One variety of Chickweed has pretty flowers, and is not as invasive as the Common Chickweed. It makes a good plant in the perennial garden, growing best in a shaded location.

The Chickweeds attract many of the smaller butterflies such as the Blues, Coppers, and Hairstreaks. A butterfly that prefers the nectar of the Chickweed is the Falcated Orangetip. Found throughout the eastern United States, except for the extreme south, the Falcated Orangetip resembles the Sulphurs in that it is white, however the male Orangetip has orange on the tips of the forewings. Both wings are bordered in black dots. The underside is quite beautiful with a background of white with a nearly fifty percent covering of brownish-orange dots and pale orange streaks ending in black dots on the edge of the wings. The green chrysalis appears as a thorn on the stem of a plant. One butterfly that eats the Chickweed is the Dwarf Yellow.

Stellaria media

CHICKWEED

WINTERGREEN

Wintergreen is the one of our best known evergreens. This tiny shrub grows to three to six inches tall from creeping stems. The leaves are oval with obscure teeth, with the white, waxy bell-shaped flowers hanging beneath them. This plant is found over the entire eastern United States in forested situations, particularly in pines.

In years past, the Wintergreen, also called Checkerberry, was harvested for the flavoring that could be added to candy and gum. Every school child knew the delight of chewing the new leaves during the spring or of eating the bright red berries during the fall or winter. The older leaves would give the same wintergreen taste but with an added bitter taste. A brew of tea would be made from the fresh-picked leaves to cure the winter aches. However, dried leaves lose their oils through evaporation, rendering them useless.

Many natural landscapers are now using this ground-hugging shrub as a natural cover for areas beneath pines and other trees. A good nursery or garden center should be able to obtain these plants for you. As they will colonize, the purchase of few Wintergreen plants will give you a good start.

The berries are relished by birds and animals alike. They are particularly loved by chipmunks and partridges. Deer will paw through the deep snow to reach the leaves.

The flowers of the Wintergreen are preferred by a number of bees and wasps. Hummingbirds will attempt to take nectar from them, but because of the Wintergreen's closeness to the ground they are usually not successful. The chipmunk is probably the greatest fan of Wintergreen, as it eats both the berries and the flowers. A couple of Leaf Miners attack the leaves during the summer and fall, but are not especially harmful to the plant.

Gaultheria procumbens

174

WINTERGREEN

SQUIRREL CORN

The Squirrel Corn grows in the eastern United States down to the Carolinas. It is similar in appearance to the Dutchman's-breeches. The Squirrel Corn has numerous white, heart-shaped flowers that hang down from a flower stalk. The leaves of this six-inch plant are very dissected, appearing fern-like and lacy. This spring wildflower is a woodland denizen, blooming early before the leaves of the trees block out the sun.

When found together, the Squirrel Corn and Dutchman's-breeches are called Boys and Girls. The Dutchman's-breeches represent boys with breeches, and the heart-shaped Squirrel Corn represents the girls. The name, Squirrel Corn, comes from the roots, which have small tubers that resemble kernels of corn. These can easily be seen as they are often at the surface of the soil.

The roots of the Squirrel Corn can be used to start new plants. It can be challenging to collect the seeds of the Squirrel Corn and propagate the plant from the seeds. The flower stalks remain above the dissected leaves and make tiny, heart-shaped capsules. You must not wait too long to harvest these seeds, as they will die back with the plants at the end of the summer and be lost. As the seed capsules begin to dry out, the seeds should be collected and placed in a container with moist moss, unless you are going to sow them shortly. The seeds will not germinate unless they undergo a cool, dormant period. Therefore, sowing should be done in the fall so the winter will prepare the seeds for best germination.

Although it is not as easily grown as the Spring-beauty, the Squirrel Corn is a good addition to the shady parts of our yard as an early spring wildflower.

Dicentra canadensis

SQUIRREL CORN

DUTCHMAN'S-BREECHES

Related to the Squirrel Corn, the Dutchman's-breeches has a raceme of waxy, white flowers. These flowers have two large spurs that point upwards, giving the impression of breeches hanging on a line with a belt of yellow. The two spurs of the blossom are that to which the genus *Dicentra* (two-lobed) refers.

This eastern woodland wildflower blooms in rich forest situations, before the trees get their leaves. Dutchman's-breeches can be found as far south as northern Georgia.

After blooming they produce their seeds and die back. The flowers grow to about three-quarters of one-inch long, and the entire plant to a height of about six to eight inches. The leaves are highly dissected, giving them a fern-like appearance.

Dutchman's-breeches and Squirrel Corn can hardly be told apart when they are not in bloom, except by the roots. The roots of Dutchman's-breeches are white, while the roots of the Squirrel Corn are yellow like a kernel of corn. When found together these flowers are called Boys and Girls. The Dutchman's-breeches represent boys with breeches, and the heart-shaped flowers of the Squirrel Corn, the girls.

The flower end of the Squirrel Corn, Dutchman's-breeches, and Bleeding Hearts are very similar. Because the flowers are closed at the end, not too many insects visit the flower. Some butterflies such as the Coppers, Blues, and Sulphurs are attracted to these flowers. The Blues may also use this plant as a food source. Sometimes, a Robber Bee will cut through the outer petals of the flower to get to the inside. Bees and bumble bees pollinate the flowers as well, but because of the shape of the flowers, they have a difficult time obtaining nectar.

A spring woodland wildflower garden is the perfect place for these plants. They spread easily and are readily available from most garden centers and catalogs. The wild seeds can be harvested and the plant propagated from seed if you have patience.

Dicentra cucullaria

DUTCHMAN'S-BREECHES

BONESET

In the same family as the Joe-Pye-Weed, the Boneset has the same dense set of white flowers borne on the top of the plant in flat clusters. The leaves make the Boneset easy to identify. They are opposite, and unite at the stem to give the impression that it is one leaf. The leaf completely surrounds the stem and is said to be perfoliate like the Bellwort.

The plant, including the leaves, is very hairy. Boneset grows in the moist soils of marshes, ditches, and shorelines, and can be found throughout the entire eastern United States. Boneset is a summer plant and it blooms from mid-summer until the first frost.

Probably no herb has had as many cures credited to it as the Boneset. According to the Doctrine of Signatures, the plant heals bones the best. One cure for which it was famous was for a disease called "break bone fever." A tea concocted from the leaves could cure anything from rheumatism to lethargy.

Boneset is not used in the home garden, but some prairie species are used in natural gardens. Some butterflies like the flowers, but they are not all that popular with hummingbirds who seem to prefer brighter-colored flowers. During the winter it is of some benefit to birds as it holds its seeds above the snow.

The Boneset is one of the special marsh flowers that attract a variety of butteflies. Three butterflies that are attracted to the Boneset are the Great Spangled Fritillary, Painted Lady, and Yellow Swallowtail. If you wish to see any of these butterflies, just spend a little time in a marsh during the months of August and September. Hummingbirds are also abundant at this time of the year, as the young are moving about and preparing for their southward migration.

Eupatorium perfoliatum

BONESET

PUSSYTOES

The Everlastings include flowers in the composite group that keep their flower head shape and last a long time without much attention. Included among these are the Pussytoes, Cudweeds, and Pearly Everlastings.

The Pearly Everlasting is the most showy of these and is ardently collected for fall dried flower arrangements. They can grow up to two feet tall, with the flowers being about one-quarter inch across. Unlike the many asters and flowers of the composite group, the Pearly Everlasting and Pussytoes do not have ray flowers but creamy-white petal-like bracts. The stem and underside of the leaves of Pussytoes are cottony. This adds to its beauty for dried flower arrangements. The leaves of the Pussytoe are lance-shaped, lying alternately on the stem. The Pussytoes differ from the Everlastings by having a basal rosette of leaves.

Pussytoes is not cultivated in the home garden, but it would be a welcome addition. The Pussytoes enjoys dry soils. Although it is not as prominent in the south it can be grown there, except in the extreme southern parts. Some types of Everlastings or Pussytoes can be found nearly everywhere.

The flowers of the Pussytoes are not exceptionally attractive to many butterflies as a nectar source, but this plant makes a good food source for the American Painted Lady and Painted Lady butterflies. The larvae of these two butterflies prefer this plant, although it seems the Painted Lady butterflies are somewhat diverse in their food plant selections. On occasion, some of the small, open meadow butterflies may visit the Pussytoes, but not readily. The Pussytoes does not need fertilization to produce a seed, so attracting pollinators has not been a big priority.

Antennaria plantaginifolia

PUSSYTOES

PARTRIDGEBERRY

Even though the Partridgeberry can be found all over the east, it is more common in the northern wooded areas. This vine can grow to several feet and become a mat. The opposite leaves are quite small, about one-half inch in diameter, shiny, and have white veins in them. The flowers are fused at the base, giving them the name Twinflower, and are four-petaled, with corolla tubes behind the petals. The petals are fringed, and range from white to pink in color.

After the flowers are pollinated, usually by butterflies like the Painted Lady, Copper and Fritillary, a double, bright red fruit is produced with two blossom ends, which appears to be one berry. These berries can be eaten, and were used by Indians for food and medicine. The leaves were used to make a tea that cured everything from the cough of a cold to whooping cough. A tea made from the berries or leaves was used to hasten childbirth and make labor go smoothly.

The Partridgeberry prefers acid soil and shade. It makes a good ground cover as it mats and only reaches a height of a couple of inches above the soil. It will grow well under pines and other evergreens where other ground covers have trouble. This plant is easy to transplant or it can be obtained from your local garden center. Many people use the Partridgeberry in small terrariums because of its small leaves, evergreen quality, and the nice color of the bright red berries.

Wildlife loves the berries as indicated by the name. The berries remain on the plant until the next growing season, so are available to birds and animals all winter long.

When planting the Partridgeberry in the home landscape, it can be combined with plants that do not require a lot of light. It makes a good ground cover for ferns, Jack-in-the-Pulpit, and Foam Flower. The Partridgeberry will survive well in little light, and the red berries will add accent to the deep green foliage of the ferns and mosses.

Mitchella repens

PARTRIDGEBERRY

185

BEDSTRAW

Bedstraw flowers are clustered at the top of the plant and at the leaf axis of the upper leaves. This plant grows about two feet tall, and has whorled leaves which are lance-shaped and parallel-veined.

This common plant of the East is found in rich soils of shores, woodlands, and waste places. Bedstraw blooms all summer long, producing seeds with hair-like hooks that transport them. Although quite pretty in the wild, this plant should remain there as it can be invasive and take over more attractive species.

Bedstraw acquired its name from the practice of using it to stuff mattresses. It worked well as a stuffing because the stems did not become brittle and turn to powder. Bedstraw also remained together as a mat because the leaves and stems are covered with tiny, hook-like hairs which attach themselves to each other and prevent the stems from moving around. Because of these characteristics, this plant is also know as Cleavers.

A juice extracted from the Bedstraw was used to curdle milk and make cheese. Being related to coffee, the roasted seeds make a fairly good coffee substitute, some say even better than Chicory. The plant was utilized as a spring green when young. Bedstraw was also used to make a brew to cure various illnesses and as a red dye.

The flowers of the Bedstraw are very tiny, so do not provide a lot of attraction to bees and butterflies. As with humans, the early spring shoots are eaten by wildlife such as chipmunks, white-footed mice, and partridge. In the fall, the seeds are sometimes eaten by migrating birds such as the Towhee and White-Throated Sparrow. The seeds are also collected by chipmunks and mice for the winter.

Galium boreale

186

BEDSTRAW

YARROW

Yarrow is sometimes mistaken for Queen Anne's Lace in its early growth because it has the same kind of fern-like leaves, except the leaves of the Yarrow are even finer and lacier. The leaves of this perennial are alternate, and the flowers are produced as a flat cluster at the top of the plant. The individual flowers have a number of ray flowers that surround the flower center. The flower heads can reach several inches across, and the entire plant grows to a height of two to three feet.

The Yarrow is a welcome immigrant from Europe and is found over the entire eastern United States, except for the lower half of Florida. It grows in a variety of conditions, wherever the soil is not too wet or disturbed. In the garden, the Yarrow is adaptable to most soil conditions.

Woundwort is another name given to Yarrow because of the ability of its crushed leaves to stop bleeding and infection. The crushed leaves even smell like the disinfectant Listerene.

This plant has been highly hybridized to give varying colors including reds, purple, yellows, golds, white, and violet. The wild plants have been harvested for years, and dyed to enhance dried flower arrangements.

Because Yarrow is such a nice plant to have in the perennial garden, it can be worthwhile to try to propagate it from seed. After the flowers have stopped blooming, keep track of them for about a month. The seed heads should become brownish and fat, indicating the seeds inside are ripe. Collect the plants and hang them upside down to dry for a week or two. You may wish to put a basket under the plants in case some seeds fall out. When the plants are dry, the heads should be crushed with a rolling pin. Mixed in with the chaff will be found the tiny seeds of the Yarrow. A bit of chaff will not hurt the seeds. The dry seeds should be stored in the refrigerator for a month to allow them to become viable. The seeds should be sown the following spring.

Achillea millefolium

YARROW

DAISY FLEABANE

The Daisy Fleabane is similar to the Asters. It is a composite with ray flowers surrounding the tiny, central, yellow flowers. The ray flowers may be white, pink, or even faint blue in color.

The Daisy Fleabane grows about three feet tall with flowers being about one-half inch across. The leaves are hairy, alternate, and lance-shaped, with very prominent teeth. It grows in waste places, meadows, roadsides, and old fields. This Fleabane is one of the first to bloom in the spring, beginning in May and perhaps lasting until fall.

The name Fleabane refers to this plant's reputation for preventing fleas on animals and people. Supposedly this plant, when crushed in the hand and rubbed over a dog, would rid it of fleas.

Because the flowers of Daisy Fleabane are not extremely large or the plants very bushy, it has not been a popular cultivar. However, allowed to grow naturally, it is beautiful. Some commercial wildflower mixtures add the seeds of the Daisy Fleabane to their packets because they are easily grown and will reseed themselves.

Being one of the first composites to bloom in the spring, it seems reasonable that this plant would have a host of larvae that would make it their food plant. However, this is not so. The only larva that eats the Daisy Fleabane with any regularity is that of the Geometer Moth, which eats the flower petals of the Daisy Fleabane. However, many butterflies make the flower of the Daisy Fleabane a source of nectar, among them the Sulphurs, Crescents, Tortoiseshell, Painted Lady, Adminals, Blues, and Coppers.

Erigeron annuus

190

DAISY FLEABANE

OX-EYE DAISY

By far the most common daisy, the Ox-Eye Daisy is found over the entire eastern United States in the dry soils of old fields, meadows, pastures, and roadways. It gets its name from the deep, yellow center surrounded by up to three dozen bright, white petals. The flower can be over two inches wide. The leaves are dark green blades with deeply indented teeth, with rounded edges instead of sharp points. This Daisy can grow up to three feet tall.

An immigrant from Europe, the Ox-Eye Daisy is not palatable to cattle, and therefore is found extensively in pastures. When accidentally eaten by cattle, this plant gives their milk a bad taste.

The Ox-Eye Daisy blooms throughout the summer and probably is the flower that originated the "She Loves Me - She Loves Me Not" game, in which the outer ray petals are picked while repeating "She Loves Me, She Loves Me Not." The last petal remaining supposedly decided the fate of the inquirer's love life. An astute person could rig the results by knowing the ray petals are mostly odd in number. Depending on how the relationship was going, the outcome could work out your way.

The use of prairie plants in the garden is becoming more and more popular, making Ox-Eye Daisies wonderful plants for a bed or border. They grow easily from seed harvested from the wild or purchased from your local garden supply store. This perennial requires little care and spreads easily by rhizomes to provide a pretty bed of summer flowers.

The Ox-Eye Daisy, and other meadow wildflowers, attract many insects. The honeybee has a heydey in the meadow during the summer, as do the many butterflies. Among the butterflies which visit the Ox-Eye Daisy are the Sulphurs, Red Admirals, Skippers, Monarchs, Fritillaries, and Tortoiseshells. A variety of predatory insects often lie in wait under the flower of the Ox-Eye Daisy to capture unsuspecting butterflies and insects. Two of the most successful are the Assassin Bug and the Flower Spider.

Chrysanthemum leucanthemum

192

OX-EYE DAISY

FALL WHITE ASTER

The Fall White Aster is one of the most common of our fall flowers. It is sometimes called the White Heath Aster, and since it blooms during the last part of the growing season it has also been called the Frost Aster. It takes a very heavy frost to kill the flowers of this plant, and even then if the seed heads have formed, the plant remains erect during the winter.

The Fall White Aster can be found throughout the entire eastern United States, growing in dry meadows, fields, roadsides, and disturbed soils. The asters hybridize readily and so can be difficult to tell one from the other. A field of White Asters are very welcome to the eye and seed themselves naturally.

This flower is about one-half inch in diameter and the white, sometimes tinged with pink, petals surround a yellow center. The leaves are simple, lance-shaped, and short on stiff branches. The plant reaches about three feet in height.

Asters belong to the composite or Daisy family. The Asters provide a variety of color in the fall and attract a lot of insects, especially honeybees. During the winter, the plants provide seeds for wildlife, especially birds, as they stay erect above all but the deepest snows.

In the fall, as flower production begins to fall off and bees and butterflies are scurrying around anxiously seeking nectar, the Fall Asters become quite important. The Anglewings and Question Marks are two of the most prominent butterflies to visit the Aster. The fall migration of the Monarch is also helped by these flowers as they make their way south to Florida. Although at this time of year, the Sulphur Butterflies are starting to decline in population, they are still quite prominent in the Asters. Grasshoppers and some of the stink bugs will also make use of the Fall White Aster as a good food source before the arrival of winter.

Aster pilosus

194

FALL WHITE ASTER

MAYWEED

Mayweed is one of the first daisy-type plants to bloom in the early summer. It has white blossoms with yellow centers, somewhat reminiscent of the Daisies in the fall.

This European weed is easily identified by its lacy, thrice-cut leaves. It has spread throughout the United States and grows to about one foot in height in dense beds. It begins to bloom in June, when it is at its best, with some plants blooming as late as early fall.

Mayweed is part of the Chamomile family and the leaves give off a bad scent when they are crushed, giving rise to the name Stinking Chamomile. Yet another name for Mayweed is Dogfennel. The Chamomiles are known for being very strong in their odor and taste. Chamomile tea is made from this group.

The Mayweed also has a bad odor, which causes numerous insects to seek out the plants for protective purposes. The Mayweed appears to exhibit some type of growth inhibitor, which discourages the growth of nearby plants. Numerous plants protect themselves by doing this. This habit allows the plants not to have to worry about competition from nearby plants. In the garden, it is wise to become aware of which plants do this so as not to cause some favorite plants to be damaged.

Mayweed likes to grow in moderately rich soil with a moderate amount of moisture. Other than the growth inhibiting factor, which can be planned for, there is no reason for this plant not to be included in a garden landscape. However, it is rarely, if ever, used.

Anthemis cotula

196

MAYWEED

BUNCHBERRY

The four white flower petals of the Bunchberry are really white bracts. The true flowers are small, yellow, and located in the center of the white bracts. The six-inch plant has a whorl of six oval leaves with occasionally a couple beneath the top whorl. Plants that do not produce flowers or the bright red berries only grow four leaves in the whorl. Because the flower is a member of the Dogwood family it is sometimes called the Bunchberry Dogwood.

The Bunchberry is a plant of the cool, northern forests, and so is not found far south, except for in the southern mountains. This flower blooms from late spring into the first part of June. The bright red berries are said to be edible, but the berries of the Wintergreen are preferred. Deer and other forest animals like the berries as well.

Although it is difficult to transplant, the Bunchberry is a welcome addition to an acid pine understory. The leaves remain green throughout the winter, and offer a striking contrast to the red berries. The Dogwood-like flower is very noticeable during spring. Many good nurseries are now offering this plant in pots which can be easily transplanted. Once they are established, they will spread by roots, and provide a unique and special shade ground cover.

The Bunchberry Dogwood has unique leaves. If you were to break the leaf across the mid-vein and pull it carefully apart about an eighth of an inch, you will find small, white threads at every vein still holding the leaf together. Also, the veins arising from the mid-rib head toward the edge of the leaf, but keep turning away as they come closer to the edges. In doing so, they become smaller and smaller until they disappear before reaching the edge of the leaf. These characteristics are unique to the Dogwoods.

Cornus canadensis

BUNCHBERRY

PEPPERGRASS

The flowers of the Peppergrass are very small and found on many stalks at the top of the plant. The characteristic four-petaled, white flower of the Mustard family is evident. The alternate leaves are lance-shaped with teeth. The basal leaves have a large terminal lobe, and can have as many as five or six other smaller lobes. Often, as the plant blooms and produces seed, the basal leaves die back.

Peppergrass is found throughout the eastern United States along roadsides, in old fields, and fallow farmland. Poor-Man's-Pepper is a common name for this mustard of the field.

The Mustard, or *Cruciferae*, family is noted for the unique seed pods they produce from the four-petaled flowers, and many are used commercially for oils or food. Even though the Peppergrass is not used commercially for flavoring it has been used in the past as a pepper substitute.

The wafer-like seeds can be harvested as soon as the flower petals fall for flavorings in salads or they can be dried. The young leaves have been used as greens in the early spring and as a salad garnishment.

The Peppergrass plants can also be dyed and used in dried flower arrangements. They remain quite stiff and can be harvested until snowfall. The plants readily accept clothing dyes, and can therefore be made quite attractive.

The Cabbage White and Creamy Marblewing butterflies use the Peppergrass plant as a host plant. The Cabbage White butterfly is a serious pest in commercial plantings of cabbage and related plants.

Some wildlife will use the seeds during the winter, so one should not be too hasty to till under the plants. Peppergrass is not used in the home landscape.

Lepidium virginicum

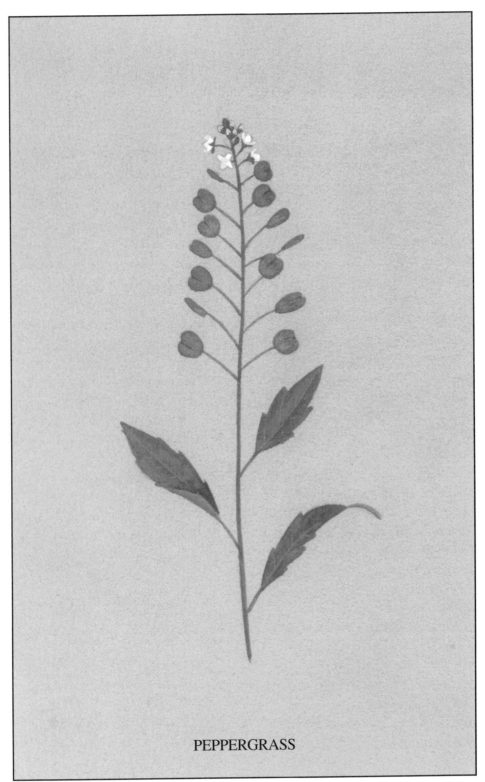

PEPPERGRASS

ENGLISH PLANTAIN

This European weed and its relatives are the scourge of the gardener. It grows profusely wherever the ground has been tilled, or where man has disturbed the soil. This gives rise to the Indian name, White Man's Footprint. It was not prevalent before the white man began cultivation.

Found everywhere, this weed is characterized by long, lance-shaped leaves growing from a cluster at ground level. The bushy, dense flower head is produced on a long, grooved spike. The actual flower is white, or greenish white, and very tiny. In the suburban yard the flower heads, sometimes called "bucktails," are distracting and distressing. They return a flower head within a day of lawn cutting. So annoying are these bucktails that years ago a special tool was invented to cut just the bucktails without cutting the lawn again. Today they are controlled by herbicides. The Common Plantain, having wide leaves and a long flower head, is also quite a nuisance.

Europeans and immigrants highly prized these plants for the nutrition they could get from using them as greens. More nutrition can be gotten from the plant than from Chard or Spinach. Another popular use was that of making compresses and poultices from the leaves. It was thought that the leaves would draw out any poisons and infections.

Probably the prettiest butterfly that uses the Plantain for its food plant is the Buckeye. This butterfly is a soft brown all over with orange patches and edges. It also has cream-colored 'eye spots' which may deter predators. When resting the Buckeye resembles a dried leaf. The Buckeye is common over the entire eastern United States. An examination of a number of plaintain leaves should reveal the caterpillar of the Buckeye. Other butterflies that use the Plaintain for food are the Checkerspot, Baltimore, Fritillaries, and Sulphurs.

Plantago lanceolata

ENGLISH PLANTAIN

POKEWEED

The Pokeweed has many names: Inkberry, Poke Salad, Pokeberry, Pigeonberry, and Poor Man's Asparagus. This tall plant, reaching over ten feet, is found over the entire eastern United States in meadows, roadsides, fields, and edges. It blooms from July through September.

The small quarter-inch flowers are clustered together like grapes on stalks, separate from the leaves, and near the end of the plant. The five white to greenish petals are really sepals that appear petal-like. The leaves are long, oval and smooth. The stem is easily identifiable because it is quite thick, succulent, and reddish in color.

The plant is used as a substitute for asparagus when just emerging from the ground. It should be boiled thoroughly in a couple of water changes before eating. Once the plant begins to leaf out the stems, roots, and berries are said to be poisonous.

Indians and early settlers used the berries for dye and ink, giving rise to the name Inkberry. The dried leaves also made a yellow dye used by the Indians.

In today's world, the Pokeweed is used very little as a spring potherb. What is recommended today is to eliminate the plant where were find it because of the poisonous qualities of the entire plant: leaves, berries, stems, and roots. Even though the berries are used by wildlife for food it is not practical to take a chance if small children are in the vicinity.

While cross-country skiing, you may run across this plant with its purple berries still intact, and the snow beneath a purple blotch. Freezing seems to make this plant more palatable to some wildlife.

Phytolacca americana

POKEWEED

SHEPHERD'S PURSE

Shepherd's Purse is one of the Mustard family, and has the characteristic four-petaled flowers. The flowers, however, are hard to see as they are quite small, growing on a long terminal stem. The leaves are arrow-shaped and clasp the stem. The basal leaves can be quite divided, appearing much like Dandelion leaves. This European weed is found everywhere in fallow ground and waste places. The plant will virtually grow any-where if given a chance.

The seed pods are triangular with an indentation at the end giving them a heart shape. The flowers and, ultimately, the seeds are born on one spike at the end of the plant. Occasionally, this plant will be confused with the Peppergrass, and the seeds do have a similar taste

This plant is interesting because it blooms virtually the entire growing season. The flower spike just keeps growing to ac-commodate new flowers until frost. Seeds, flowers, and newly forming buds are all found on the same spike.

As in the Yellow Rocket, the Olympia Marblewing uses the Shepherd's Purse for a source of food. Another butterfly that utilizes the Shepherd's Purse for food is the Falcated Orangetip. As you may have guessed, this butterfly is white with orange wing tips on the forewing. It also has black spots that border the wing's edge. The underside of this butterfly is the prettiest part. It is a pearly white with bands of orange, brown, and gold. The chrysalis is green and appears as a small leafy appendage next to the stem.

Capsella bursa-pastoris

206

SHEPHERD'S PURSE

SOURCES FOR WILDFLOWER GARDENING: BOOKS AND VIDEOS

Attracting Birds to Your Backyard With Roger Tory Peterson, Video, Michael Godfrey. Nature Science Network, Carrborro, NC.

Attracting Butterflies to your Backyard, Video, Michael Godfrey. Nature Science Network, Carrborro, NC

Audubon Society Handbook For Butterfly Watchers, Robert Pyle. Johns Hopkins University Press, Baltimore, MD

Butterfly Garden, Mathew Tekulsky. Harvard Common Press, Boston, PA

Handbook for Butterfly Watchers, Robert Pyle. Houghton Mifflin, Boston, PA

How to Attract Hummingbirds and Butterflies, Ortho Books. Chevron Chemical Co., San Ramon, CA

Hummingbird Book, Donald and Lilian Stokes. Little, Brown, Boston, PA

Hummingbird Garden, Mathew Tekulsky. Crown Publishing, New York, NY

Landscaping For Wildlife, Minnesota Department of Natural Resources. Minnesota Natural Resources, St. Paul, MN

Landscaping With Wildflowers, Ortho Books. Chevron Chemical Co., San Ramon, CA

Landscaping With Wildflowers, Jim Wilson. Houghton Mifflin, Boston, PA

Nursery Sources: Native Plants and Wildflowers, New England Wildflower Society. Framingham, MA

Suburban Nature Guide, Richard Schinkel and David Mohrhardt. Stackpoll Press, Harrisburg, PA

Wildflower Book, Donald and Lilian Stokes. Little, Brown, Boston, PA

Wildlife Gardener, John Dennis. Alfred A. Knopf, New York, NY

Wildflower Meadow Book: A Gardeners Guide, Laura C. Martin. East Woods Press, Charlotte, NC

Wildflowers of Indiana, Maryrose and Fred Wampler. Indiana University Press, Bloomington, IN

SOCIETIES AND ORGANIZATIONS

Illinois Native Plant Society, Department of Botany, Southern Illinois University, Carbondale, IL 62901

Lepidopterists' Society, 257 Common Street, Dedham, MA 02026

National Wildflower Research Center, 2600 FM 973 North, Austin, TX 78725

New England Wildflower Society, Hemenway Road, Framingham, MA 01701

Operation Wildflower, Central Atlantic Division, 2513 Raven Road, Wilmington, DE 19810

SOURCES FOR SEED AND PLANTS

Alternative Groundcovers, P.O. Box 49092, Colorado Springs, CO 80949

Applewood Seed Company, 5308 Vivian St., Arvada, CO 80002

Bluestone Perennials, 7211 Middle Ridge Road, Madison OH 44057

Clyde Robin Seed, P.O. Box 2366, Castro Valley, CA 18974

Green Wellies Garden Shoppe, 111 N. Main, Berrien Springs, MI 49103

Iverson Perennial Garden, Box 2787 RFD, Long Grove, IL 60047

Lilypons Water Garden, 6800 Lilypons Road, Buckeystown, MD 21717

Natural Garden, 38 West 443 Hwy 64., St. Charles, IL 60175

Nichols Garden Nursery, 1190 North Pacific Hwy., Albany, OR 97321

Prairie Nursery, P.O. Box 306, Westfield, WI 53964

W. Atlee Burpee Gardens, 300 Park Avenue, Warminster, PA 18991

Wildseed Farms, 1101 Campo Rosa Rd., Eagle Lake, TX 77434

GLOSSARY

alternate: arising singly on a stem, not across

annual: living only one growing season

anther: pollen-bearing part of stamen, male

axil: upper surface of union between leaf petiole and stem

basal: located primarily at base of plant

biennial: a plant that requires two growing seasons to complete its growing cycle

bract: a very small or modified leaf growing at the base of a flower or flower cluster

bulb: an underground bud with scaly or fleshy layers

calyx: the outer circle of flower parts made from sepals

clasping: leaf partially surrounding the stem

composite: daisy family of flowers, the flower head made up small flowers growing together

corolla: the inner circle of flower parts made up of petals

compound: divided into separate smaller parts

disk: the central, round part of the daisy family flowers, usually with small flowers in the center and ray flowers on the outer edge

doctrine of signatures: a theory that parts of plants held "signatures" that resembled parts of the human body and that plant would benefit that body part medicinally

irregular: when parts of a flower or leaf are of different size, shape, or location

lance-shaped: broader at one end tapering to a point, much longer than wide

leaflet: one of the smaller parts of a divided or cut leaf

lip: the upper or lower part of an irregular flower

lobe: an indentation that is rounded on the outer edge

oblong: longer than broad with parallel sides, not lance-shaped

opposite: occurring on the same position on a stem across from each other, a pair

oval: egg-shaped, rounded but one end wider

palate: projection of the lower lip of an irregular flower

palmate: divided so leaflets radiate from a central location, as fingers of a palm

perennial: living for many seasons, more than one or two

preflight: leaf clasping stem entirely, stem piercing leaf

petal: one of the segments of corolla, showy part of flower

pistil: the central female portion of the flower, comprising the ovary, style, and stigma

pinnate: divided so segments are divided on each side of a stalk, may be opposite or alternate arranged

pod: fruiting part of fertilized flower

pollen: spores produced by the anther, male

raceme: a long cluster of flowers on a central stalk

ray: in composite or daisy family, petal-like blades that encircle the disk of central flowers

rosette: a circular cluster of leaves at the base of a plant, basal

sepal: one of the segments of the calyx, modified leaf near flower

sessile: without a stalk, arising directly from stem

simple: without dissection or lobes, not cut, whole

stalk: stem of leaf or flower

stamen: male portion of flower, top has anther which produces pollen

terminal: at the end

toothed: having several pointed indentations on the edge of the leaf

trailing: running across the ground as opposed to erect

tuber: a short thick under ground root with buds

umbel: an umbrella-like cluster of flowers where all the stalks are palmate

whorled: three or more leaves arising from a central point

wing: a thin, narrow membrane or flap growing on a stem or a stalk of a plant

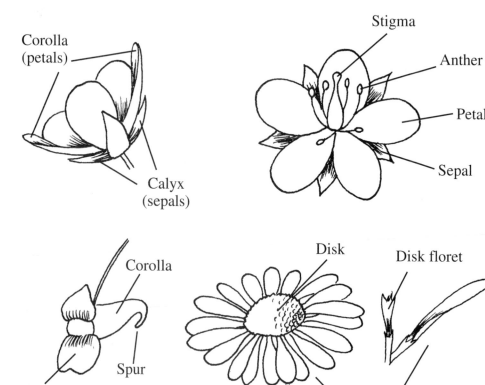

Corolla
(petals)

Calyx
(sepals)

Stigma

Anther

Petal

Sepal

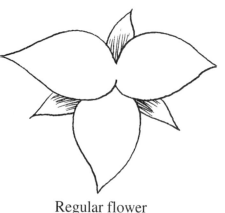

Corolla

Spur

Lip

Disk

Disk floret

Ray
flower

Regular flower
(radially symmetric)

Irregular
flowers

PICTORIAL GLOSSARY

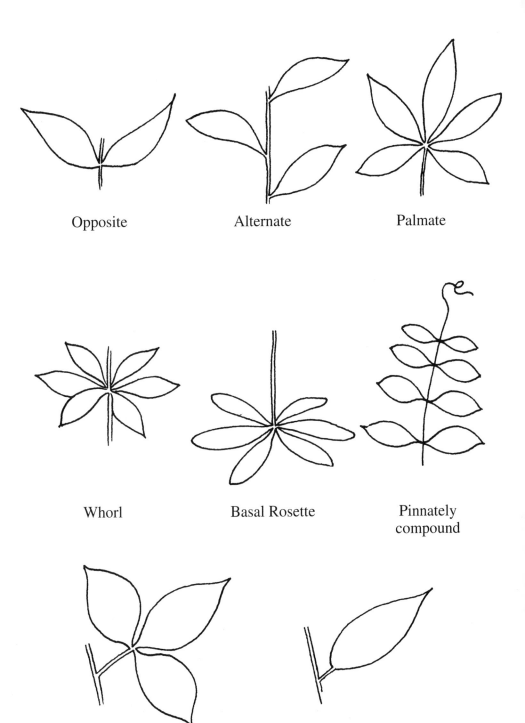

Opposite

Alternate

Palmate

Whorl

Basal Rosette

Pinnately compound

Compound

Simple

PICTORAL GLOSSARY

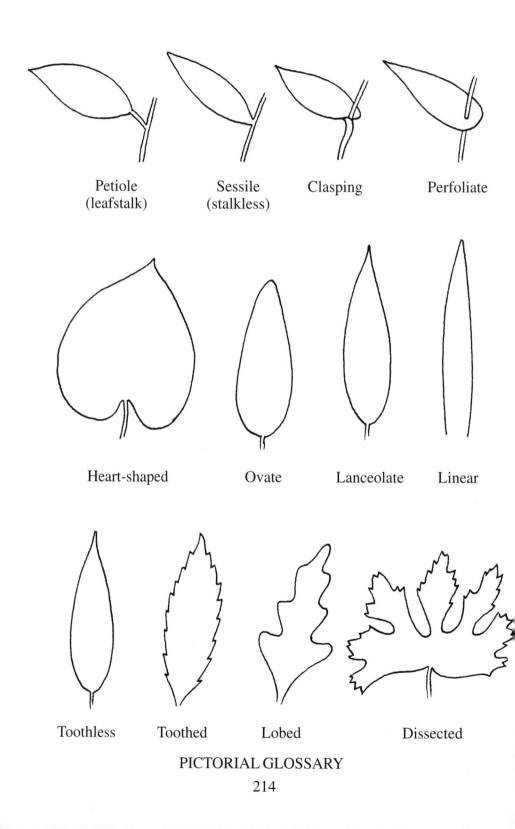

Petiole
(leafstalk)

Sessile
(stalkless)

Clasping

Perfoliate

Heart-shaped

Ovate

Lanceolate

Linear

Toothless

Toothed

Lobed

Dissected

PICTORIAL GLOSSARY

INDEX

216